MW01232231

God's
Ultimate Love

may God's Blessings overflow over you

Betsy Beck

B E T S Y   B E C K

PAGE PUBLISHING, INC.
New York, NY

First originally published by Page Publishing, Inc. 2019

ISBN 978-1-64424-664-1 (Paperback)
ISBN 978-1-64424-665-8 (Digital)

Printed in the United States of America

My prayers have always been to be able to help hurting, abused women to find their identity in Christ Jesus.

I have ministered at Christian Women's Job Corps for five years in Guntersville, Alabama. It has been an awesome blessing to see so many ladies' lives be changed.

I have ministered in my home for eight years, at my church, and at Mercy Home. I have seen many tears and heard so many cry about how unworthy they are.

I pray this book will help many more to know God is only in the future; that after Christ there is no past, only today, no yesterday; that the past is so far gone they will never have to travel it again. In Christ, there is only new life.

I want to acknowledge Jan Young for her time and encouragement but, most of all, her friendship and love.

The Most Rich and Blessed

We are the most richly blessed of people that have ever lived. If we can grasp the message Jesus brought to us and stand firm and establish it in our lives, we cannot stumble. Our steps are ordered by the Lord. His Word is our pathway to His righteousness. Our life has been prearranged. If we will live in His Word and put it first over anything and anyone, we will not be defeated. We need to know that we are in the world but not of the world. We have His Spirit in us and are sprinkled daily with His blood.

We have to give Him our best sacrifice and apply His Word as food daily, or we will surely die. His Word is our peace and rest; it is our meat. The Bible is spiritual food for the souls. Our soul has to be fed like our body. When we nibble at the desires of the flesh, we lose sight of God's desires. Worldly ways may satisfy our soul for a while, causing us to wither and die spiritually. We must cast down the demons that take our peace and joy. When David had a battle to fight, he would tell his enemy, "I come in the name of the Lord."

It is time for repentance and seeking God's will and dying to ourselves. Ask God to take away the things not pleasing to Him and fill us with Himself, letting our cup run over. Fix your eyes upon Jesus, the author and finisher of our faith. He, for the joy set before Him, endured the cross and has sat down at the right hand of the throne of God. Consider Him, who endured such much hostility so that we may not grow weary and lose heart by the Holy Spirit. His love has been perfected and completed in us. He has given all of us His special gift, but we must walk in God's love.

He speaks of never becoming puffed up. If we become puffed up, we begin to walk in pride, and this in turn leads to arrogance. If we are arrogant, how can we walk in love with our brothers and sisters in Christ? I believe this is a commandment from God—to love your neighbor as yourself. We are to not be a respecter of persons but should treat everyone the same whether they be poor or rich. We are to love one another and never make our brother or sister look small in someone else's eyes. This is the way we will bring unity into the church.

As Joshua fought the battle at Rephidim, Moses stood atop the hill with his hands raised, and his hands got heavy. Aaron and Hur helped support his hands. We, too, are to hold our brother's and sister's hands up during their battles. We are to hold each other up in prayer and stand in the gap for them when they are weak and can't stand. We are not to gossip about our brothers and sisters. We all have skeletons in our closets. Don't bring judgment on yourself by pulling someone's skeleton out from under the covering of the blood of Jesus. Sometimes we need to share something we've gone through, but don't backbite if someone puts their trust in you. Walk it out with them, lifting them up in prayer and helping them keep it under the blood of Jesus.

We shouldn't pass judgment down on others by the words spoken from our mouth. Never speak evil of others, for that which you've spoken will fall upon you. The seeds we sow are the seeds we harvest. Trust me. I have harvested a few, so I know this to be true. Ask the Lord to increase their faith and release them from their bondage and help you walk in love. Most of all, we must pray for one another. We need each other, and we need to help them not feel rejected.

When a man has been rejected, he seeks power for himself. It is very important to let someone from the beginning of their childhood know that they are loved and needed, keeping their spirits and values focused on who they are in the kingdom of God. Assure them they are important to God and us. I believe if we teach them God's values and help them keep the Word of God before them, it will help them adopt a way of life that will always be effective to them. If we do that, they could become powerful workers for the kingdom of God along their journey in life. Oh, what peace and joy would rest upon them.

If we fill them with their weaknesses, it would open the door for the enemy to steal the vision God has for them because he loves to tear down a person's self-confidence. We need to keep fear and doubt from our children at all times. Fear, anger, and rejection walk hand in hand with the enemy in the lead. They will have no self-esteem without God as their Savior, leading to destruction for them. We are to be examples for them. If you are always raising your voice in anger, it will cause them to be hard of hearing, so how can they believe God is love?

Yes, children need discipline but with a firm and loving voice. We need to use the rod, but not in anger. When I do something wrong and God needs to get my attention, He never raises His voice, but He speaks with firmness. I can always feel His love. We can treat our children in such a way that will bring insecurity, causing them to lust for attention, in turn demanding man to know "I am worthy of being loved." The insecurity of being unloved will bring determination to be noticed and self-centeredness in turn opening the door for Satan to enter their mind and emotions, which start the attack of destruction. I read in a Bible study that a child doesn't have to be taught dishonesty but has to be taught the truth. We need to ask God's blessings on our children, asking Him to guide us in teaching our children. He will not let you down.

We are all His family, and He values family. He established a covenant in order to protect his holy union. He is always attentive to His sheep. We are God's vessels. It is our prayers that keep safety around us. We are to take authority over the thing of which He has put us in charge. Jesus took back what the devil stole. He took back the earth. God's Word says he gave the world to the children of man, and that is us!

Satan has no power over us! The sooner we learn that one thing, the more understanding we will have about the authority Jesus gives us through His name. Jesus is the one that conquered, and we've been given a higher authority in the name of Jesus!

We are the seed of Abraham; we are the harvest reapers. Deuteronomy 15:5–6 reads, "Only if thou carefully hearken unto the commandments which I command thee this day. For the Lord thy God bless thee, as He promised thee: and thou shalt not borrow; and thou shall reign over many nations, but they shall not reign over thee." If God made Abraham one of the most blessed men in the Old Testament, will He not do the same for His children in the New Testament?

God will take us through our battles. He may have to take us the long way for us to triumph, but He will get us to His destination. He may have to take us the long route to keep us from having to fight a battle we won't win, but He will walk beside us and make sure we do win. He knows where our battles are to be fought. It may be in the lion's den, but we will come out as Daniel did.

The king asks Daniel, servant of the living God, "Has your God, whom you consistently serve, been able to deliver you from the lions?" Daniel then said to the king, "O king, live forever and ever! God sent His angel and shut the lion's mouth, and they have not harmed me." God will send you an angel to shut your lion's mouth. For whoever is formed of God shall overcome the world.

We will serve someone; it will be God or the devil. One thing we know, if we serve the devil, we won't have much of a battle. He will make it easy for us so that we will not become discouraged and run toward God. He can deceive us if we so easily let him. Yes, he can give us riches and fame on this earth, but one thing I promise you, if you choose to serve Satan, when your life here on earth is over, there will be no rewards or crowns.

When our enemy blinds us, we need to pray as Elisha. Look how God helped him win his battle. "He said 'Fear not; for they that be with us are more than they that be with them.' And Elisha prayed and said 'Lord, I pray thee, open his eyes that he may see.' And the Lord opened the eyes of the young man; and he saw: and, behold, the mountains was full of horses and chariots of fire round about Elisha. And when they came down to him, Elisha prayed unto the Lord and said, 'Smite these people, I pray thee, with blindness.' And He smote them with blindness according to the word of Elisha" (2 Kings 6:16–18). If we knew what Elisha knew when he spoke, "Fear not, for they that be with us are more than they that be with them," we would walk in the faith of Elisha and see the victory we have over our battles.

When Elisha answered according to what he had seen with new spiritual eyes, the battle was over. To be able to see like Elisha would cast out doubt and fear. His eyes beheld the horses and chariots of fire that were sent to rescue from God on high. His prayers were answered through his faith. I submit to you the faith of Elisha.

The moment his eyes were opened, he thought not of himself but of the people. He commanded the blindness to come upon the enemy, and instantly the blindness manifested. When we get our vision on the true mission of Christ, our prayers are not hindered but automatically answered. How many of our prayers go unanswered because of our lack of faith?

Mark 11:23 reads: "For verily I say unto you, that whatsoever you shall say unto this mountain, Be thou removed and be thou cast into the sea; and shall not doubt in his heart, but shall believe that those things which he says shall come to pass; he shall have whatsoever he says." We need to pray and fast for God to give us spiritual eyes so we will know that they that be with us is more than they that be with them.

Once we accept the fact that we are the blessed children of God and receive the calling he has put upon us, the faith of Elisha will stir up inside us, and we will have boldness in Christ. No longer will we allow the enemy to walk anywhere near our camp.

I believe that before the battle, the Holy Spirit will warn us and prepare us. Faith in Christ can create in you a new beginning, a new walk of boldness and oneness with Jesus. You will say, "I am consecrated, set apart. I have God's unmerited favor, peace, harmony, and unity. Through the blood of Jesus, I have redemption, deliverance, and salvation. I have forgiveness of my offenses, shortcomings, and trespasses in accordance with the riches and generosity of His gracious favor, which He lavishes upon me in His will, plan, and purpose. In Him, I obtained God's inheritance. I choose to live for the praise of His glory! He has made me alive together in fellowship and union with Christ. He gave me the very life of Christ, the same new life with which He quickened Jesus. It is by His mercy and favor that I am saved and delivered from judgment. He that raised us up together with him made us to sit down together, giving me joint seating with Him."

Our salvation is not based upon what we can do but upon what Jesus gave for us. When the enemy comes against you, he deceived you by getting your focus on your righteousness. All deliverance comes by asking God to reveal the sin in our life, repenting, and submitting to God. Surrender all desires and yield to His authority and power with a true heart and be totally honest with Him; therefore, you've left nothing uncovered.

Take time to seek and search His Word, and treasure it in your heart. Let your heart see the deep secrets of God, and reveal all your secrets to Him. Know that your sin has been atoned and removed as far as the east is from the west. We no longer have to live in sin, shame, and fear, and death has chains on you no longer. "So when the corruptible shall have put on incorruption, and this mortal shall have put on immortality, then shall be brought to pass the saying that is written. Death is swallowed up in victory. O death where is your sting, O grave, where is thy victory? The sting of death is sin; and the strength of sin is law" (1 Corinthians 15:52–56). We now know we no longer live in sin. The Father has put His mark on you—the blood of Jesus. That is the only thing that edifies you to the Father. We can know we have a clean conscience before the Father. We can now go into the holy of holies and worship with a true spirit and heart.

God is waiting for us to surrender to Him, beginning our march. If we, the body of Christ, will join together and pray, fasting for our loved ones and our country, we will see change. We need to stand at the gates and keep the demons and the old serpent out of our cities.

Jesus was sent to the earth for a purpose, which He fulfilled. We are all to preach the gospel, to set the prisoners free, and to heal the brokenhearted. We have to take our stand in the Word of God. He took back the earth and gave us a higher authority through the name of Jesus. The harvest is not in the church; it is outside the church. He may ask us to do some things that don't make sense. He asked Moses to lift up his rod and stretch his hand out over the sea. When he obeyed, the waters parted.

The enemy will try to put pressure on you. He puts the heat on you and will turn it up so high you can hear the crackling of the flames. But we have power within us, which is called the Holy Ghost, to fight against what the devil does. There are people dropping into hell every day. For those who remain, we have the words they need to hear. We have the love within us they are looking for—the love of Jesus. We have to lead them to repentance and the love of Jesus.

When God's children are slothful in spreading the gospel of Christ, other means are used. Scripture reminds us the rocks will come bold with the message of salvation and peace. The message is released, and then the receiver has a choice to make. Minister to those in need, but do not hinder, argue, or demand. Christ doesn't command that we receive salvation; it is a free gift. He gives us the choice—to choose life or death. We should live a life that permeates His presence, a life that attracts people on a daily basis, a life full of joy that others will want to know the secrets we have. When doors are opened, explain the source of your joy, and tell of the gospel of Christ.

The Lord promised to save the lost. We only have to be His mouthpieces. He said we shall lay our hands on the sick and they shall be healed, so we have to be His hands. He said He would pour out His Spirit upon us, but we have to be ready when He calls. Live the life that Christ demands. Diligently seek His face to guide and direct your path. Allow God's gifts and comfort from the Holy Spirit to dwell in you and emit from His power in you a glow that the world must declare the source.

The Bible reads in Romans 14:11–13: "For it is written, as I live saith the Lord, every knee shall bow to Me, and every tongue shall confess to God." So every one of us will give account for the life we have lived. Let us therefore not judge one another and not be a stumbling block to others. Man must not continue to fall short in building the life that God could use for the full effect of Jesus's shed blood.

Man is a dwelling place for either the Holy Spirit or evil spirits; two cannot dwell within the same body. It is up to man to decide for whom he is building a dwelling place. There is one catch—you cannot use the same blueprint for the dwelling place of the Holy Spirit and evil. You must use the plans established by the master builder, the Word of God. All instructions are there for us. We must ask the master builder to explain the blueprints. The blessings of God are in the house of a righteous man. How you choose to build your house is how blessed you will become. The plans, God's Holy Word, have been tested through the ages. Choose which house you want to build—good or evil.

In these last days, we should be taking part in the great celebration, the outpouring of the Holy Spirit. The great revelation for God's children has come. We have to arise and shake ourselves, seeking insight as to what field we are to harvest and put on the whole armor of God. Be prepared for war, having your feet shod with the preparation of the gospel of peace. Be fully prepared to say, "Lord, here I am, send me." Our God has delivered us from Satan's snares. He redeems from everlasting hellfire and damnation into eternal life in Him. We gain adoption turning away from unrighteousness in order to serve the true Living God.

As Daniel prayed morning, noon, and night for God to prevail, He did. He will do the same for us when we pray in faith with a pure heart. Deny ungodliness and worldly lust in order to live soberly, righteously, and godly in this present time. We are to be strong in faith with a humble spirit, putting on mercy, kindness, humbleness of mind with meekness and long-suffering.

Know that no matter how sinful, unrighteous, and hopeless a person seems to be, Jesus loves them just as much as He does you and me. Jesus said in John 6, "He that heareth the Word and believe on Him hath everlasting life and shall not come into condemnation but is passed from death into life."

We are to never let ourselves be caught up in envy of spiritual gifts. Never let anyone beat you down with jealousy, keeping you from walking in the gifts God has given you. Every part of the human body is important. The little toe even controls part of our balancing process. It is the Word of God that keeps us balanced. You have been given a holy gift; treat it with honor and respect. Never pervert your gift by using it to glorify yourself; use it to glorify the kingdom of the Giver.

God has called you to be a laborer during this time of harvest by first planting a seed. The spiritual gifts you possess will allow you to call upon the supernatural ability to serve in a capacity you never dreamed possible. Allow the Holy Spirit to instruct you according to the time, place, and manner in which you are to plant or serve. Consecrate your gifts to God and His service before action, and then continue to pray for the watering of the Word upon your seed. The harvest will soon come; your fruits will become evermore evident, and God will be edified from the wheat produced. We have to grab hold of our ministry. God has set aside the godly for Himself; we are His.

What an awesome God we serve! He is mercy and strength, never leaving us alone. He gives us the confidence and assurance that He will help us through any trial. He leads us out so we can help someone else through their trials. If we didn't go through troubles, how would we be able to help someone else? Help them to know. "Call upon Me in the day of trouble," God says in Psalm 50:15. "I will deliver you, and you will honor Me."

It is time for God's people to wake up and know what Jesus's death on the cross and His resurrection did for us. It's time for us to know who we are in Christ Jesus! We have to understand that God has made a promise to us. It doesn't matter which way we turn. His Word will not lie, it will prosper.

God is calling us to be prepared at all times, having our lamp full of His oil, filled with the Holy Spirit. He is a fountain of living water that springs up and flows out. He has to flow out before we can be fruitful. You can't empty out if you're not full. We have to be prepared to set the captive free. There are so many hurting people out in the world today. We are His witnesses and His mouthpiece.

When God puts us in ministry and we move out in faith, there will be no stumbling blocks in your path. God doesn't give us secrets about Himself for us to keep it all to ourselves. He wants us to give away what He gives us so He can fill us up again. He will put us in the right place at the right time. He will put the person you are to share with in your path. When we answer His call, we will be fruitful. When we sit at the devil's table and feast upon the desires of our flesh, feeding it a little at a time, we lose sight of God's desires and His plans for us. We have to be prepared at all times, staying full of His Word. His Word fills up the empty spaces, closing the door to the enemy.

He is calling us into unity. It doesn't matter what color we are, whether black or white, red or green. We as Christians have to learn that we have the same Father. We are all in a covenant. In God's covenant, we are as one individual. It is a covenant to accomplish God's plan.

Our salvation was established on the cross. When Jesus walked up Calvary's hill, dragging the cross, it wasn't the weight of the wood He carried on his back; it was the weight of our sins, sickness, and lack that made up the weight. When He picked up the cross, He said, "Come on, Betsy, my child, I bring you salvation." He picked me up and put me on His back; it was me He carried. Our God is totally committed to us. Beyond a doubt, we consume His time.

We have let man take our eyes off the cross. We can't see the cross anymore because of the words that are being spoken by man. You know it's true by what has been preached to us, that God doesn't heal anymore and you have to give money to receive a blessing. Our life is all about the cross, so when we're sick, look to the cross; or if we lack, look to the cross. See yourself standing behind it. When Jesus went to the cross, He paid the ultimate price for us—His life at Calvary. He is now our Master. I know you've probably seen a movie where someone bought another person and that person became the other's master. That is what Jesus did in a sense. He is our Master, our builder.

God is so near, yet His love and mercy reaches the entire world. He is ever near but never so far away to help in time of need. He hears us, answers us, and strengthens us. This is one of His prayers: "And now I am no more in the world, but these are in the world, and I come to thee Holy Father, keep through thine own name those whom thou hast given Me, that they may be one, as we are" (John 17:11).

We are now filled with God's life through Christ Jesus. If He is for us, who can be against us? If Jesus is for us, that should give us the fullest of confidence. "Peace I leave with you, My peace I give unto you: not as the world giveth, give I unto you. Let not your heart be troubled, neither let it be afraid" (John 14:27).

When you develop a trusting relationship with Christ, you can begin to see things take place in your life. Trust must be present in both parties in order for it to be called a trusting relationship. We have a growing season in Christ. Through these trials, we get to know Christ. He teaches us His Word is true, for He is not a man that He can lie; nor will He leave us. The battle is not ours but His.

As babes in Christ, we have to start with the sincere milk of God's Word so we can grow and become fully equipped for His service. We have to have the power of the Holy Ghost in our lives to be strong and overcome. In Acts, Jesus says, "Ye shall receive power, after that, the Holy Ghost is come upon you." John 14:26 reminds us: "But the Comforter, which is the Holy Ghost, whom the Father will send in My name, He shall teach you all things, and bring all things to your remembrances, whatsoever I have said unto you." Rejoice in the comfort and power that comes only from the Holy Ghost. Daniel 12:3 states: "And they that be wise shall shine as the brightness of the firmament; and they that turn many to righteousness as the stars for ever and ever."

Our Father was so blessed by the baptism of His holy Son that He opened heaven and sent the Holy Spirit in the form of a dove. Just think about it, saints. The Holy Spirit was not revealed to the disciples until after Jesus ascended into heaven, but this same Holy Spirit now resides in us (see Acts). God could not physically touch His Son without causing major harm to those witnessing the event, so He instead did the next best thing: He opened heaven to touch and let Jesus know He was loved.

God came for His Son one other time in the Bible—when Christ gave up His Spirit to His Father. When God came for one last touch and opened the veil for us, what a great event. What a great manner of love the Father has given unto us. The spiritual darkness that the disciples experienced became light when their eyes were opened on the Emmaus Road. God knew these men needed their Savior as He knew we needed a Savior. However, He promised not to leave them as orphans, so He sent Jesus to visit and explain the presence of the Comforter, the Holy Spirit.

The Holy Spirit was intended to be the comforter of men. God used the same Holy Spirit to comfort His Son at His holy baptism. What a beautiful picture God's love painted for us. Man can receive the baptism of the Holy Spirit. How much closer we become to Christ when we receive this blessed gift.

We cannot allow ourselves to ride the spiritual fences, putting one leg over into worldly pleasures. Your salvation cannot be compromised. You must decide, declare, and decree whom you represent. All God wants is your whole heart, a pure heart, having a true relationship, not letting anything stand in the way when we accept Him. He loves you more than anyone you could love on earth. "Blessed are they that do His commandment, that they may have right to the tree of life, and may enter in through the gates into the city" (Revelation 22:14).

Satan tempted Jesus twice in the Bible. He did it with the very words of God. He quoted straight from Psalm 91:11–12. What better weapon could the enemy use against you than your own word or those said to you or about you? Jesus responded by reminding the devil of another quote from the Bible: "You shall not tempt the Lord your God." Jesus only used two weapons: scripture and immediate obedience. These two weapons are available to believers today. We must not read the Word only; we must react and obey.

The devil sends his spirits to spy on us. He uses all his resources to entangle himself into our lives as he did Jesus. One way is by listening to our prayers. Another is, he listens to how we openly speak of our situations to others. He also plants things in our mind by what we hear or what we watch. Our eyes are the windows to our soul. We all are in a spiritual battle, like it or not, and face battles daily. But I have good news for you; Jesus is the one fighting the battle for us. He goes ahead of us with His mighty sword, His Word. We have to keep our mind refreshed with His Word. We have to be refreshed in His Word daily, attending church and listening to the spoken word God has given our shepherd.

We refuel through the Holy Spirit by praying, reading the Word, and letting it drop down into our spirit. Just as we put fuel into our vehicles to keep them going, the engine must be working properly for the gas to make the engine run. Our engine, our heart, must be pure and in working order and receive the gas, which is the Word of God. Many times, we don't like paying the price of gas because it's too high. And in the same sense, we may feel the same way about God's Word, that the price is too high. Sometimes we find old spirits of hindrance, unforgiveness, or disobedience in the way. But if we let the Word of Christ become new in us and get satiated and replenished, it brings new life, and we are ready for new beginnings. People now have a new refreshed Christian to deal with. "But now in Christ Jesus you who once were far off have been brought near by the blood of Christ" (Ephesians 2:13).

A Wake-Up Call

One Saturday, a group of us from church went to witness door to door in a local community. I knocked on the door of an apartment, and a young lady who looked to be around sixteen years old opened it. I began telling her about Jesus, and as I did so, she asked, "Who?" I paused in my explanation because of her asking this question. I asked her, "Do you know who Jesus is?" She shook her head and answered no. It is hard to believe that there are people in this day and time that have never heard about Jesus. This should be a wake-up call for us who do know Jesus Christ.

As I began to tell this young lady who Jesus was, she listened wide-eyed with much anticipation. I asked if she would like to visit our church and learn more, to which she said yes. As I moved on through the apartments, I glanced back, and the young lady was following me, listening to what I told the others. I then realized that we need to reach out more to the lost because Satan is taking our neighbors right in front of us.

They don't know about the cross. They don't know that they are fighting demons that God himself has put under our feet and stripped of their power. They don't know that Jesus died so that all could be free. They need to hear Luke 10:19: "Behold, I give unto you power to tread on serpents, and scorpions, and over all the power of the enemy; and nothing shall by any means hurt you."

I was in a revival where I know we prayed seven demons out of a young lady. After she was delivered, she wept begging her mother not to let them come back. She said the demons would come into her bedroom at night and beat her in the stomach. She said they had tried to kill her the night before. I told her it was because they knew she was going to be delivered. I will never forget the fear that was in her eyes. Later in the week, I thought, *How can we help others be delivered if we haven't learned who we are in Christ?*

I believe that 9/11 was a wake-up call for America. For a while, people fell on their knees, but they didn't stay there, seeking God daily. This is the same God that Noah served. He still hates evil and sin and is a jealous God. As I look around, seeing so much violence, I think of Genesis 6:5–7: "And God saw that the wickedness of man was great in the earth, and that every imagination of the thoughts of his heart was only evil continually. And it repented the Lord that he had made man on the earth, and it grieved him at his heart. And the Lord said, I will destroy man whom I have created from the face of the earth; both man, and beast, and the creeping thing, and the fowls of the air; for it repenteth me that I have made them." It is time we take our place and stand for our country. I believe we don't have much longer before the Father tells the Son, "Go get my bride. The earth is corrupt."

When we read the paper or watch television, we can see the flesh is corrupt. Revelation says in the last days the spirit of Sodom and Gomorrah will be upon the earth, and I believe it is upon the earth today. Before the second coming, there will be a rapture of the saints. Once the rapture takes place, the events written of in Revelation will take place expediently. There is so much about the day of the Lord that people do not know. The day of the Lord refers to all events after the rapture. "Let no man deceive you by any means, for that day shall not come, except there come a falling away first."

We were followers of the course and fashions of the world, following the prince of power of the air. We were obedient to and under the control of demon spirits and then…Jesus. We are by nature children of God and joint heirs of His indignations. Because of His intense love for us, He sent His only begotten Son to die on the cross so that we could have eternal life. Jesus delivered us from the principalities of darkness, from Satan. He has set us in heavenly places.

We are His creation in whom He loves. He made provision for us. He made a way out for us. We are the reason for the cross. There is no way to escape death except through Him. His Word tells us in Isaiah 44:6–8: "Thus says the Lord, the King of Israel and His redeemer, the Lord of Host. I am the first and the last, is like Me? Let him proclaim and declare it; yes let him recount it to Me in order, since I appointed the ancient people. And are you My witness? Is there any other God beside? Or is there any other rock? I know not one." These words are straight from God, and we can't deny them. He is the only way to eternal life. John bears witness of him crying out, saying, "This was He whom I said, he who comes after me has a higher rank than I, for he existed before me" (John 1:5).

Salvation is a gift from God. We have to turn our hearts to God, turning our hearts to truth, justice, and righteousness. We have to come out of the darkness. I was thinking of the phrase I've heard: "the darkest hour is before dawn." The Holy Spirit spoke to me and said, "The darkest hour isn't before dawn. It will be standing before Jesus on judgment day and not having received Him as your Lord and Savior." Jesus became sin so that we wouldn't have to go through this darkest hour. The moment we receive Him as Lord, our darkest hour becomes light.

We are now in Christ, a recreated spirit. His Word tells us that we are hidden in the Father through Christ Jesus, so when the storms come, where are you? The Word tells us that Jesus conquered the world and stripped it of its power so it can't harm us. Never let us faint or waver, but know that Jesus is the way of life. He still carries the wounds that should give us the assurance He made all things possible for those who love Him. He keeps us under His garment. He walked in the greatest darkness so that we could walk in the "greatest light." He died so that I could be free and help someone else become free.

We are God's chosen witnesses to proclaim before Him. There is no other God formed; neither shall there be after Him. He is Lord, and there is no other Savior. He is our Redeemer, the Holy One of Israel, our King! From the promise to Abraham and God's covenant with him, his seed at a thousand generations stands today; we are that covenant seed. What God has spoken He will bring to pass. What He has purposed He will do! He hears, answers, and strengthens.

When you are going through valleys, think of the gifts He gives: love, joy, peace, deliverance, and most of all, eternal life. When we look in the mirror, let it be His reflection you see. He gives us the end of our faith. What I am saying here is, stand firm in Christ and experience the maturity.

He told me that faith brings hope, hope brings roots, and roots keep us firmly planted. He gives us the end of any circumstance at the beginning. There is no circumstance. It is only His Word sustained and replenished.

We belong to Him. He allowed us to be birthed into this world for a purpose. Jesus had a mission; it is to destroy the works of the devil. We, being on the same mission, must let His light shine through us, exposing the works of darkness, the works of Satan. There is a harvest of lost souls to save to gather in these last days. His Word tells us that the sinners are waiting to hear what we have to say. We must labor, for their blood will be on our hands. I know we've heard this all our lives, but the reason stands for repeating is because we are not receiving.

I know we become weary and tired at times; I want to tell you Jesus is faithful. He will bring us out of our midnight hour if we, like Paul and Silas, begin to shout off the chains. "My yoke is easy and My burden is light" (Matthew 11:30). "'Fear not for I am with thee," says the Lord our God (Isaiah 43:5). Facing these so-called problems with the eyes of Christ will bring everything into focus. The attack of the enemy never catches our God asleep. "Behold, He who keeps Israel shall never slumber nor sleep" (Psalm 121:4). We must be prepared when the enemy comes and not let him inside the gate. We must always keep God's Word alive in us, for this is the foundation we build upon. If we walk by faith, He will take care of us.

I love to read the story in Mark 10:46–52:

> And they came to Jericho and as he was going from Jericho, with His Disciples and a great multitude, the son of Timaeus, was sitting by the road. And when he heard that it was Jesus of Nazarene, he began to cry out and say, "Jesus, son of David, have mercy on me!" And many were sternly telling him to be quiet, but he kept crying

out the more, "Son of David, have mercy on me."
And Jesus said, "Call him here," and they called
the blind man, saying to him, "Take courage,
arise, He is calling for you." And casting aside
his cloak, he jumped up, and came to Jesus. And
answering him, Jesus said, "What do you want
Me to do for you?" And the blind man said to
Him, "Rabbi, I want to regain my sight." And
Jesus said to him, "Go your faith has made you
whole."

I believe Jesus is asking us the same question today: "What do you want Me to do for you?" How far can your faith carry you?

I was talking to a friend about how Jesus would heal us. She let me know she didn't believe that. She was like her daddy, who had known many men who died in the war. She had known many Christians who died from sickness. So what kind of God was that? I thought for a moment what I should say when the Holy Spirit quickened me, saying, "It is the faith within you that makes you whole." If there is no faith, there is no healing, no hope, and no eternal life. Jesus is all this; he is the reward of those who seek Him.

It is so vital to read His Word aloud each day, letting it drop down into your spirit. What we feed our spirit is what we become. Whom we hang out with is who we will become. If we walk in Christ, we are made more than conquerors. I can truly say that I have never known a Christian who hung out with sinners and won them to Christ. It has always been the other way around; the Christian returns to the sinful life.

Hebrews 10:22 reads: "Draw near with a true heart, with assurance of faith. Having our hearts sprinkled from an evil conscience and our bodies washed with pure water, let us hold fast the profession without wavering. For He is faithful that promised." If we are unknowledgeable in God's Word, Satan has the ability to put blinding spirits over our eyes about the authority Jesus gave us. He gave us authority in His name over our enemy. He gave us dominion over the earth. He made us in His image, His likeness. We are made to be conquerors; even as He, so are we.

I was fasting, and on the last day of the fast, the Lord woke me about 5:00 a.m. He took me to Psalms, where the lions looked to Him for their meat. He said, "They know my voice." He gave me a vision of a lion sitting out in a field. He said, "The lion will sit there all day, but at the first scent of his enemy, he will raise his head and the stronger the scent, the lion rises and begins to walk the field roaring telling his enemy not to come any closer, this is my domain."

He said, "My children must know that I have given authority and dominion to them through my Son's blood. They have to draw a blood line and tell the enemy not to cross the line. This is their domain in the authority given with Jesus's name." I believe God is calling out some people to take their authority over sickness and over lack in this time and season. "Truly, truly, I say unto you, he that believes on Me, the works that I do shall he do also; and greater Works than these shall he do; because I go unto the Father" (John 14:12).

I can remember as a child when I did something wrong, I was told, "The devil is going to get you." I thought at any time I would look up and see the devil coming after me. I thought the devil had as much power as God. I thank God for the wisdom and knowledge in His Word. We now know that the devil is a defeated foe and is under the feet of Jesus.

When a thief is caught, he is put into prison and no longer free. I believe the thief has been caught and no longer free to seek whom he may devour. Jesus put the thief out of business. We need to get a hold of this vision, of Satan being stripped of his power. He walks as a roaring lion, and all he can do is roar. He is only a shadow with no authority. He can only follow. When we receive Jesus as Lord, His light overpowers the shadow. By the mercy of God, we have freedom. Don't listen to the one who charges you. Be like Bartimaeus and get louder: "I have eternal life. Jesus is a lamp unto my feet. No weapon formed against me shall prosper. No lack, no sickness, shall enter into my camp."

Satan can also enter in through our speech; he loves to magnify our problems. The Word of God tells us there is life and death in the power of the tongue. We have what we say we have. Seeds sown are a harvest reaped, whether it is bad seeds or good seeds. "Idle words are idle thoughts."

The only way Satan can keep you in blindness is to keep you in darkness. No one can find their way in the dark without stumbling and falling, but once you see a ray of light and walk toward that light, you have a lesser chance of falling. That is the way it is with Jesus. He is the light that lights up the world. He is the light that will bring you out of your darkness. We cannot be free of the chains that bind us without Jesus.

Sometimes we get ourselves into trouble trying to do things our way. We get ahead of God, which brings more chains to bind us. We have to be still and wait on God. Our time is not His time, but His time is our time. Our time is "We want it now." His time is "When I know you are ready, child." He has to know we are mature enough for the assignment He has for us. Let our wait make us stronger in Him by building our faith in God, which supplies all our needs. He is our father, mother, brother, and our sister, and He is our best friend. It is His hand that rises up us each morning. We may not see or feel Him, but it is Him.

The effect of not waiting on God can bring destruction in our life and cause us to be out of His will, opening the door for the enemy to shoot his arrows. We have to be willing to give up our way, the "I want it now" mentality. We need to start tearing down everything we have built and let Jesus rebuild our life. We need to get our mind off earthly treasures and the mansions we build on earth and seek the heavenly mansions. "Seek ye first the kingdom of God, and His righteousness and all these things will be added unto you" (Matthew 6:33).

Look at yourself today as the Father sees you, covered by the blood of His Son. He can't look upon sin; therefore, He can only see the purest part of you. God sees Jesus as pure, true, and holy. Through repentance, our selfishness, impurity, ungodliness, and unrighteousness is taken away. The veil has been split, and now we can go into the holy of holies. The veil has been removed from our eyes. God can now identify you through His Son's blood.

"Seeing then that we have such hope, we use great plainness of speech. And not as Moses, which put a veil over his face, that the children of Israel could not steadfastly look to the end of that which is abolished. But their minds were blinded; for until this day remains the same veil untaken away reading of the Old Testament; which veil is done away in Christ. But even unto this day, when Moses is read, the veil is upon their heart. Nevertheless when it shall turn to the Lord, the veil shall be taken away. Now the Lord is that Spirit: and where the Spirit of the Lord is, there is liberty. But we all, with open face beholding as in a glass the glory of the Lord, are changed into the same image from glory to glory, even as by the Spirit of the Lord" (2 Corinthians 3:12–18)

The anointing issued here is to free man, not to harass, destroy, or blind. Only the devil can bring these devices upon our life. When we are in unbelief, this can blind us about our salvation and the reason of the cross, making us like the Israelites, having the veil still over our eyes. Let God arise and take control and commit all to Him.

The enemy comes to steal your vision. He knows where we are in our walk for God. He comes after your revelation, taking our minds captive so we can't stay focused on our vision. He will sit on our shoulders and daily whisper his lies if we allow him to do so, making his thoughts our thoughts. We have to rise up and know our authority. Our life is a journey to the "beginning of life." Be in control and be sober minded, and don't let his lies cloud your mind.

When fighting a battle, be like Eleazer. His hand had to be pried off his sword. What is our sword? It is the Word of God. If we don't have the Word in us, we don't have a weapon when the enemy comes. Sometimes we fight battles that don't require a man-made weapon. The greatest battles we fight sometimes are with family members, in the church, even the pastor. No matter what the battle, Jesus is the answer. "The battle is not ours. It belongs to the Lord."

Strife and unforgiveness are an open door for the devil. He loves to find strife and unforgiveness in the home or church. He knows these are tools for division, and you will have a continuous battle.

Lay it all at Jesus's feet and shout down the victory when you have gone as far as you can. When we praise God, I believe we are making cracks in the wall of the enemy's camp. We are to do as Jesus looking down at his enemies on the cross; He prayed, "Father forgive them."

One of the strongest weapons we can use on our enemy is love. When we attack our enemy with harsh words, we're opening the door for the enemy to bring another battle. Love overpowers the stronghold. When we sacrifice our flesh and deny it power, it will put the enemy asunder. Love conquers all things because it is Christ in us. "For if you do not forgive men for their transgressions, the Heavenly Father will not forgive you of your transgressions" (Matthew 6:15). There's only one way we can get the attention of God the Father, it is through the blood of His son.

When we refuse the devil's weapons and receive God's weapons of love, forgiveness, peace and joy, this will bring deliverance and freedom. If we let the enemy in, he can bring distraction causing us to fail Christ. A tree can only produce fruit of its own kind. We cannot be light and darkness, for we can only serve one master. God has separated you for Himself. He desires to have your whole heart, a heart that truly abandons everything in order to yield itself to the authority and power of the Blood, a heart that chooses the "new life" that He has chosen for us. Christ has made us a descendant of a heavenly kingdom. He has made us His ambassador and governor. We are to convert our garden into the image and likeness of His kingdom.

Proverbs 29:2 says, "When the righteous are in authority, the people rejoice, but when the wicked beareth rule, the people mourn." When we don't take authority over the enemy, we are doing as Adam and Eve and letting the serpent enter into our garden. We have to recognize our enemy and put him out before he has time to play games with our mind. We have to quit fighting the same battle over and over; we have to win the battle, getting victory over it. If we keep fighting the same battle, we lose ground, and the enemy becomes stronger, soon consuming us. We must walk out of the battle, holding up the banner of victory. We have to take our authority, which is the power or right to give commands, enforce obedience, take action, or make final decisions. Take dominion over your territory! We are to enforce the petitions made by Jesus.

The Word of God tells us that there is madness (insanity) inside of man. If the devil can enter a door that's been left open, he can torment you; he leaves no rest. Satan sees in us what he knows he will never be, and that's "victorious." He knows he has already been tried and convicted; he's already been sentenced.

Anytime you let sin creep into your life, you're giving place to the devil. Some of his main tools are fear and deception. We cannot let fear overpower us, for it brings doubt. Soon you'll be blinded and find yourself in a place where you can't get out. You are magnifying the devil, making him equal to God in your mind. The devil was only a praise angel in charge of the music; he is not all knowing. We have to stake our claim, letting him know we're on holy ground, where he is not allowed. Don't let your mind be the devil's playground. Satan will never have victory over us. Cast every anxiety upon God and commit to Him; let Him be your refuge. Have an honest heart before God. Keep it manicured by repenting daily.

Remember that Jesus became sin that we might become righteousness. It is through Jesus that we have the victory over our battles. He will not send us out without covering us. "He is in control." We can do nothing without Him, but with Him, we win. When Job was walking through his battles, God asked Job if he wanted to argue with the Almighty. He said, "Shall he that contendeth with the Almighty instruct him? He that reprove God, let him answer it."

> Then Job answered, "But I am vile, what shall I answer Thee? I will lay my hand over my mouth. Once have I spoken; but I will not answer: yea, twice; but I will proceed no further." Then answered the Lord unto Job out of a whirlwind and said, "Gird up thy loins now like a man: I will demand of thee, and declare thou unto me. Wilt thou also disannul my judgment? Wilt thou condemn m, that thou mayest be righteous? Has thou an arm like God? Or canst thou thunder

with a voice like him? Deck thyself now with majesty and excellency; and array thyself with glory and beauty. Cast abroad the rage of thy wrath: and behold every one that is proud, and abase him: Look on every one that is proud, and bring him low; and tread down the wicked in their place." (Job 40:1–12)

I believe God was saying to Job, "There is no other god. I am He that created thee. Have I not made you in My image, My likeness?"

God gave this to me when He led me through a battle of about six months. He said, "My Son shed His blood on Mount Calvary that my children could have an abundant life. My children have not comprehended the power of My Son's blood. I hear them when they say, "In the name of Jesus," plead the blood; but where is the power that manifests from these words spoken? They know not that when these words are spoken, His blood is brought back before Me."

"Worthy is the Lamb that was slain to receive power, and riches, and wisdom and strength and honour, and glory and blessing" (Revelation 5:12). He bore all your shame, all your sin on the cross. It is Jesus that makes me and you worthy to receive these things.

Religion would have you think I'm a sinner saved by grace, but I am as filthy rags. First, don't think of yourself as any part of sin. By the blood, you are no longer a sinner; you are no longer as filthy rags because you have been washed in the blood of the Lamb. Where the nail scars once brought His holy blood, that blood now brings life abundantly, light where there was once darkness. You are made in the image of the Almighty God, in His likeness; you are of a royal family. It is true that without Jesus, we are nothing, for Jesus did it all. He crowned you with glory and honor. John 12:26 says, "If any man serve Me, him will my Father honor."

Our life will never change until we begin to walk as His Word tells us, "Created in His Image, His likeness." He has given us authority and dominion over our domain to rule over our circumstances and to walk in all knowledge of God. He gives us dominion over all the arrows the enemy shoots at us so much that the tips will not even prick our skin. It is this lack of knowledge that keeps us from being successful. When you know without a shadow of doubt who you are in the blood of the Lamb and His name, you will begin to live the privileged life you are entitled to. Ephesians 6:24 says, "Grace be with all them that love our Jesus in sincerity."

I firmly believe if I'd been the only one in this world, God would still have sent Jesus after me. He didn't just send Jesus to walk through this earth. He sent him after you and me. God said, "Go get my people out of bondage." I can envision the Father saying to Jesus, "Son, I need you to do something for Me." And as Jesus lifts his head until their eyes meet, He says, "Okay, what do you need me to do?" The Father tells him, "I need you to go to the earth and get my children out of bondage, but I need to let you know what will happen to you. You will be birthed from a woman named Mary. You will become the Messiah, but they [the people] will not receive you as their Messiah. They will beat you, pull out your beard, spit upon your face, and uh… Son, they will nail you to a cross." For a moment, Jesus hesitates as He has a vision of a lost and dying world.

We were set before Him. He had a vision of people in hell and begins to mourn, for there is so much love within that He thinks His heart will explode. His head rises in admiration, and He says, "When do I go?" And He came, bringing us a flawless salvation, the escape from death. He announced the kingdom of God. He was the perfect government sent by God to convert this colony earth into His image, His likeness, representing the Father.

It is true we also have to deal with an abundance of adversity, but knowing who you are in Him and you are highly favored and created in His image and is more than a conqueror, Jesus will carry you out on the other side without harm. Remember what we learned about a kingdom—once the king chooses you, it puts a demand on the throne for your provision and safety. So when the king, our Father God, chose you, we became a citizen of a heavenly kingdom. Because of the blood shed of His Son, Jesus, it puts a demand on the throne that Jesus sits upon. We can now confess, "I am precious in His sight. He has His eyes upon me, and I am the apple of His eye." Because of our faith in God, we should dare to have the boldness, the courage, and the confidence enough to rejoice over any need in our life. We can rejoice because we have free and unreserved access to approach God without fear, no matter what our need.

Satan would love to sift us as wheat. He knows he can't cross the bloodline; if he did, he would be saved. He wants to keep your faith weakened, for he knows that out of our belly flow rivers of living water. He knows as it is in John 15:5–6: "I am the vine, ye are the branches. He that abided in Me, and I in him, the same bring forth much fruit: for without Me, ye can do nothing. If a man abides not in me, he is cast forth as a branch, and is withered and men gather them and cast them into the fire. And they burned." If we could grasp the power of the cross, oh, what power would manifest on earth!

One thing I learned going through my trials is, we are God's children and that no matter what battle we have to fight, He is our shield. There is no other god formed, nor shall there be after Him. He is the God of Abraham, and He is the God of Jacob and Isaac, so is He my God. I have learned to look to God alone for my deliverance, to look only to Him for answers. It is through the wilderness we grow. It is in the valleys that we rise up like a rose and bloom, where the water flow brings it to blossom abundantly. In every valley, you will bloom into full power and strength.

> Therefore having been justified by faith, we have peace with God through our Lord Jesus Christ. Though whom also we have access by faith into the grace in which we stand and rejoice in hope of the glory of God. And not only hope but glory in tribulations, knowing that tribulation produces perseverance and perseverance character: character, hope. Now hope does not disappoint, because the love of God has been poured out in our hearts by the Holy Spirit who was given to us. (Romans 5:1–5)
>
> And when I passed by thee, and saw thee polluted in thine own blood, I said unto thee when thou wast in though blood, live: yea, I said

unto thee when thou wast in thy blood, live. I have caused thee to multiply as the bud of the field, and thou hath increased and waxed great, and thou art come to excellent ornaments: thy breasts are fashioned, and thine hair is grown, where as thou wast naked and bare. Now when I passed by thee, and looked upon thee, behold, thy time was the time for love; and I spread my skirt over thee, and covered they nakedness: yea, I sware unto thee, and entered into a covenant with thee, saith the Lord God, and thou became mine. Then washed I thee with water; yea, I thoroughly washed away thy blood from thee, and I anointed thee with oil. (Ezekiel 16:6–9)

The word *covenant* means to fetter, chain together. With God, we become a part of this covenant to accomplish God's plan. Our salvation was established on the cross. Are we still wandering around the same mountains? Do we still not know the Lord's ways? We need to ask Him to help us receive His Word in full understanding in order to benefit His kingdom, not just to make our life easier. Every purpose of life is accomplished because of the cross. I know I have been in the wilderness for longer than forty years, for I haven't found the deep parts. He said, "If you will seek Me, you will find Me." There are deeper parts to Christ we have yet to walk in. If so, we would see the miracles. We still haven't found Him in His Majesty.

Let us see ourselves as He sees us. All sin removed and lifted up on the cross. We were forgiven of all sin in the person of Christ Jesus. His death accomplished it all. It is through His love we can walk in this deep part. We have to search our heart daily through God's Word and have a true heart. How long will it take us to see who we are in Christ? How long before He can come and take His bride home?

Jesus loved us so much He gave all He had, His life. He travailed for us in the Garden of Gethsemane. We were the joy set before Him. When He went into the garden, He prayed, "Father, remove this cup from Me." Then He prayed, "Not my will be done, but Thine

Will be done." He became impregnated with our salvation. His labor pains were for us to be born again unto salvation.

Jesus knew what He had to do in order for us to be restored back to the Father. He knew He must shed His blood to atone. He knew He would bring us a love from His Father that we could never be separated from. He had heard from the Father and knew He would not lie. He knew God is true, holy, pure, faithful, never changing, and all powerful. He knew He had to die that we might live.

He is a seed brought forth through Mary to produce and bring forth life. We have to die to our flesh in order to get to the Father. He chose us; we did not choose Him. He knows our name; He calls us beloved. Everything since the creation of time has been about the Father. We are always on His mind and in His heart. The more anointing He pours upon us, the closer we get to Him. He will never deny our cry for help. He made us a blessing for Himself; never exalt yourself. Don't forget who you are in Him. We cannot do anything without Him, but we can do all things through Him. He demands our faithfulness. Know that "greater is He in me than he in the world."

The way we walk in freedom is walk in the truth of Christ. Once we know these truths, freedom will come. There is a dying world outside our walls, so let our light be the light of Jesus, shining and overpowering the darkness. Some of the richest treasure given can be the Word of God helping someone be free of their yokes, their bondage.

Never Stop Marching

God is always attentive to our needs. His plan for our life is never at a standstill. He loves to find ways to please His children; He loves to bless us and give us gifts. If we become satisfied with our walk, we open the door for the enemy to keep us from walking in the gifts God has given to us. When we become satisfied with simply holding on, we can let the devil come in and invade our everyday walk and bind our march of victory over our battles. We cannot stand still. We must keep on walking!

We are recreated in Christ Jesus, but if we listen to the devil's lies, we will never march again. God's Word tells us to walk in His kind of love to endure long, be patient and kind, never to be envious or jealous over each other's gifts. Love each other even as you love yourself. We must keep our march, for now is the time and season to proclaim the coming of the Lord, bringing forth His gospel to a dying world.

We are to rejoice when right and truth prevails. We are to be peacemakers. We are destined and appointed by God to become progressive in knowing His will for our life. We must be submissive to God, always putting Him first in our life. We have to stop seeing ourselves in weakness and start seeing ourselves in His majesty, clothed in the area of His light and covered in His blood. We must walk out of the wilderness totally dependent upon God. We must walk in a path of perfect submission and obedience, at all times trusting in Christ. We have to get up out of the grave of woe and despair of our past and see ourselves as the bride of the royal priesthood. Jesus has paid the price for us to walk in His likeness, so we need to let go of our past and step over into our new life as a new creation and be more than a conqueror.

God is searching for someone that will take on the garment of prayer and praise and go into battle for the lost that cry out for deliverance and go against the demons in our churches today. I believe even though Satan possesses their walk, their souls cry out to the Father for release. We are His creation and no matter what, we belong to Him. It is He that has made us, not we ourselves.

We must give ear to His words and not let them depart from our sight but keep them in the midst of our heart, for they are life and healing to our body. We must believe He sits on the throne at the Father's right hand, making intercession for us. For those who do not believe the full scripture (Mark 16:16), they are condemned.

The Bible tells us that in the last days, the heart of the people will grow cold, that it will be "as in the days of Noah, so shall it be in the days of the Son of Man. They did eat, they drank, they married wives, they were given in marriages, until the day Noah entered into the ark, and the flood came, and destroyed them all. Likewise also as it was in the days of Lot; they did eat, they drank, they bought, they sold, they planted, they built; But the same day that Lot went out of Sodom it rained fire and brimstone from Heaven, and destroyed them all" (Luke 17:26–29). Look at the destruction that has come upon the earth today. Maybe God is trying to show the world that something is about to happen. It is time to get up and call a Solomon's fast and cry out to God for America!

I was in my devotion, reading God's Word, and suddenly a spirit of unworthiness fell upon me. I leaned over the arm of the chair where I sat and began to pray, "O Father! I am so unworthy." I saw in my spirit realm the devil sitting across my shoulders, and he was beating my head on the altars. Sweat popped out on me, and I started to feel sick. Suddenly in my spirit, I heard Jesus begin laughing at me, and He said, "Are you through?" Then I begin to laugh with Him and said, "Well, I guess." He said, "Now let me show you something." I turned and picked up my pen and began writing. "Don't go to God in doubt and unbelief. Go to Him in the way He sees us, through the blood He shed for us." When we go in unworthiness, we are denying the deliverance the cross brought us. Go to

Him in truth, believing He paid the price for all things that concern us. He has called you unto Himself and has predestined our lives.

Be persuaded that neither death nor life, nor angels, nor principalities, nor powers, nor things present, nor things to come, nor height, nor depth, nor any other creature shall be able to separate us from the Lord our God, which is in Christ Jesus our Lord (Romans 8:38).

He told me we must be worshippers of God. His love for us does not change no matter what we do or how we fall. His love never changes. Even if we don't repent and go back out into the world, He still does not discard us. His love for us stays the same.

When we go before Him, let's not go with the image the devil puts before us of unworthiness and shame because we haven't prayed enough or read the Word enough. Repent and go in the image of how He sees us. Go in the name of Jesus and the blood of the Lamb! He only sees us in the blood of the Redeemer. Go to Him with a "Joyful noise. Serve the Lord with gladness. Come before His presence with singing. Know ye that the Lord He is God; it is He who made us and not we ourselves; we are His people, and the sheep of His pasture. Enter His gates with thanksgiving and into His courts with praise: be thankful unto Him, and bless His name. For the Lord is good; His mercy is everlasting; and His truth endures to all generations" (Psalm 100). When we get inside His courts, He will let us know how to pray and what His will is.

He took me to Romans 8:26–27, "Likewise the (Holy Spirit) also helps our infirmities, for we know not what we should pray as we ought. But the Holy Spirit itself makes intercession for us with groaning which cannot be uttered. And he that searcheth the hearts knoweth what is the mind of the Spirit, because he maketh intercession for the saints according to the will of God." Our prayers should come from the heart. It is His mercy and grace that sustain us. It isn't about our failures. It is about our unbelief and doubt of what Jesus did for us at the cross. It is not what we do or how we do it that makes Him love us. It is because we belong to Him; He is our Creator. Do we believe He will do what He has promised?

We have to focus upon the mighty power of our God and His capabilities. When I read in Joel about the saints coming back to the earth with Jesus, I know why the scriptures say we cannot comprehend the things He has in store for us. If we can keep our minds occupied on these things, I know there is no way we can be defeated. All I can comprehend is "Who is like Him?" There is no man like my God!

When trouble comes, do as the Word tells us to do: "Run to Him." He is our shelter, our refuge, and our fortress. If He is for me, who can be against me? (1 John 4:4).

"How great, how great is my God!" No one can take us from Him, and we are worthy because of Calvary. I know that it is the Lord that goes before you. He will march with you; He will never fail you or let you go or forsake you. Fear not; neither should you become broken (Deuteronomy 31:18). Stay in the will of God!

Many Christians today cannot walk in the will of God, for they don't know what the will of God is. They have let their time become consumed with the things of the world—work, ball games, TV, and phones. They never take the time to read the Word of God to know what His will is. I have heard people say, "If it be Thy will, heal me, Lord." It is the will of God to heal your body. Isaiah 53:5 tells us, "He was wounded for our transgressions, He was bruised for our iniquities; the chastisement of our peace was upon Him; and with His Stripes we were healed." These scriptures prove the price for my healing was paid at the whipping post. The Word says that Jesus died on the cross, which was the price paid for the redemption of humanity. So go back and read these scriptures again. He paid the price. He died for you and me. He was bruised for our iniquities. This means the suffering Jesus took upon himself was not for Him, but for you and me. He did it because of His mighty love for us.

The chastisement of our peace was upon Him. This means Adam messed up; so if the peace between God and man was to be restored, it would be Jesus's death that would build the imperishable foundation of the one and only salvation. This is the foundation to build our faith upon for deliverance of any strongholds the enemy tries to destroy us with.

"And with His stripes we were healed." Past tense. I know there are people that believe healing was only in the Old Testament. The Word of God does not grow old, nor is it dead; it is alive even today. Every time we read the scripture, we can put claim over our life, for it is the "well of God" for our daily walk. One way we can prove this is to read the New Testament about the people Jesus healed. What about the woman with the issue of blood? "Who, His Own Self bear our sins in His Own Body on the tree, that we, being dead to sins, should live unto Righteousness: by who stripes you were healed" (1 Peter 2:24).

I have had people tell me they don't believe in demon spirits. Again, what about the demons Jesus cast out of the man and went into the pigs, making the pigs run into the water and drown? God's Word is alive and active in this time and season and all seasons to come. The truth of God is what we are to build our faith upon, therefore pleasing God. "Now Faith is the substance of things hoped for and evidence of things not seen" (Hebrews 11:1). Without faith, we will never walk in the full effect of God's Word. Through Faith, we understand that the world was formed by the Word of God. God began with His Word and created all things. He took His words and mixed His faith with it and created this universe. What power!

Faith is taking God's Word and knowing no higher truth can exist. How powerful our words are if they are God's Words spoken over our daily walk. "Wherefore laying aside all malice, and all guile, and envies, and all evil speaking, as new born babes, desire the sincere milk of the word, that you may grow thereby" (1 Peter 2:1–2).

Why is it so easy for us to read a magazine or hear something on TV and believe all we hear by man, but when it comes to God's Word, we can't believe? We can't seem to take God's Word and apply it to our lives and believe it will heal our bodies and meet our every need.

I go to church with a young man who had burned his mind out on drugs. Doctors had told his parents he would never be able to function in the world by himself nor live alone again. He said God spoke to him and told him to get in His word and learn His Word. I can't begin to tell you all the scripture he can quote. He is living by himself today and driving. He goes to different schools, giving his testimony. He will tell you that the only way he exists is by bathing himself in the Word of God daily. Trust me, God's Word is life to our body. Jesus came so that we could feast of the manna of heaven. He desires that we should live life in abundance.

I was in my prayer closet when Jesus spoke to me. From the time He was conceived in Mary's womb until He ascended, everything was put in place for Him to fulfill God's Word, from the water to wash His disciples' feet to the donkey. He said, "Go and read again." He said that is the way it is for My children; all you have to do is accept His gifts and step out in His provisions and walk in them. Step out in faith and pull my mind down to the mind of Christ.

If we could only comprehend His true love for us, what power we could walk in! When we hear He gave His life at Calvary, we still can't believe He did it for us! If we did believe this, we would never get off our face. "But when the precious blood of Jesus Christ as a Lamb without blemish and without spot; who was foreordained before the foundation of the world, but was manifested in the last times for you" (1 Peter 1:19–20). If only we could come to the realization that the kingdom of God is within us; Jesus is that kingdom.

The Word of God will bring new birth within our spirit man—a new life and a new beginning. God has a deep, enduring love for us. He sent His Son to die for us. We have a heavenly Father that never takes His eyes off us. He never sleeps or slumbers. "O Lord you are my hidden place; You shall preserve me from trouble; You shall compass me bout with songs of deliverance. I will instruct you and teach you in the way which you shall go: I will guide you with My eyes" (Psalm 32:7–8). "And so we should not be like cringing fearful slaves, but the bosom of His family, and calling to Him "Father, Father" (Romans 8:15–17).

I have talked with so many people that have asked me this question: "Why are we not seeing the power of God manifested in our lives?" I try to answer them by what God has revealed to me. We have limited God to our level. We are still walking in sin consciousness and cannot receive the price of the blood of Jesus. It wasn't only the suffering that redeemed us but the giving of His body. Once again, blood has to be atoned for sin to be removed. The price of His body was the blood atonement for our sin.

"Much more then, having now been justified by His Blood, we shall be saved from wrath through Him" (Romans 6:8–9). I believe the only thing that stays on the mind of Christ is the redemption of souls. After repentance, we must see ourselves dead to all sin, past and future, by pulling our mind down to the mind of Christ. When we see ourselves as not forgiven, we are saying that what Jesus did at Calvary wasn't good enough. We are denying the power. He expects us to take the truths of His word and let it become our lifestyle. He died so that we could go beyond the physical realm and live in the spiritual realm through the Holy Spirit. "But you shall receive power when the Holy Spirit has come upon you" (Acts 1:8). This is where our power comes from. Even Jesus was limited in His physical body, but when the Holy Spirit ascended upon Him, the power was upon Him. He told His disciples, "I have much to tell you but cannot, but the Holy Spirit will tell you much more." God has a plan for you and me, and that is why He gave His Son so that the Holy Ghost would come and empower His church. We must commit to Him in all our ways and let His ways become our ways, be in His image and likeness.

After His disciples did what He commanded, the Holy Spirit came upon them. Peter then became the bold man God desired him to be. Our minds have to be made up that no matter what. We will stand for truth and justice and be rooted in His righteousness, therefore allowing the abiding presence of the Holy Spirit a dwelling place in our bodies. We have to let the Holy Spirit be upon us without measure. It is the true salvation that brings deliverance. If we don't know the true gospel, how can we minister to anyone?

"As you therefore receive Christ Jesus the Lord, so walk ye in Him, and be established in the Faith, as you have been taught, abounding therein with thanksgiving" (Colossians 2:6–7).

"For in Him (Christ) dwells all the fullness of the Godhead bodily: And you are complete in Him, who is the head of all principality and power" (Colossians 2:9–10).

The way we do this is take our spiritual authority and walk in the image and likeness of God.

Now is not the time to lay down our cross. We have a responsibility to attend to our domain and keep the serpent out of our gardens, stand at the gate of our domain and keep the serpent out of our camp. There is joy in the Lord. We have to deny ourselves as Jesus did for us, pick up our cross, receive the benefit, and never stop marching. The days of miracles are not over! The greatest days are yet to come for us. Now is the time to arise and take our place and keep marching.

One with Christ

God is faithful to His Word. His Word restores life to His people; it is creative power. Isaiah 55 is the invitation exalted to everyone—a call personally given by God. Not only does it offer water, the basic necessity of life (which is biblically the Spirit), but His Word also offers all that brings overwhelming satisfaction or abundance to life. If we believe, we become one with God.

There is a place of rest and peace in God that we find only in the Word of God, in the knowledge of knowing what Jesus accomplished on the cross. The Bible tells us: "My people are destroyed because of the lack of knowledge" (Hosea 4:6). God's Word is to the body in the spirit. What food is to the body in the natural, it is our nutrition for growth in the Spirit.

If we don't have the knowledge of God's Word, we will never know Jesus and what He accomplished at Calvary for our perfect salvation plan. We will never find the peace He paid the price for us to have. Our Faith can never grow without reading and hearing the Word of God. "So then faith comes by hearing, and hearing by the word of God" (Romans 10:17).

The Word brings joy and deliverance from anxiety and unrest. "The statutes of the Lord are right, rejoicing the heart. Your words were found, and I did eat them; and your Word was unto me the joy and rejoicing of My heart: for I am called by your name O Lord God of Hosts" (Jeremiah 15:16).

"The commandment of the Lord is pure enlightening the eyes" (Psalm 19:8). Without the Word, we are like wandering sheep; there is no direction in our life. "Direct my steps by your word, and let no iniquity have dominion over me" (Psalm 119:133). God's Word teaches us obedience. If we don't know God's Word, how can we walk in obedience? "Teach me, O Lord the way of your statutes And I shall keep it to the end. Give me understanding, and I shall keep Your Law; Indeed I shall observe it with my whole heart. Make me walk in the path of Your commandments; For I delight in it" (Psalm 199:33–35).

God's Word teaches us purity. We must live a life of holiness and purity in order to enjoy more of the Lord's presence. You can't be made pure without being cleansed through God's Word. "How can a young man cleanse his way? By taking heed according to Your word" (Psalm 119:9).

To live in the knowledge of God's Word will make your way prosperous, and then you'll have success if we live according to the teachings of the Bible. "This Book of the Law shall not depart from your mouth, but you shall meditate in it day and night, that you may observe to do according to all that is written in it. For then you will make your way prosperous, then you will have good success" (Joshua 1:8).

Deliverance will not come without the knowledge of God's Word. When we have the knowledge of God's Word, we have the image of God and His likeness, which is "authority" given to us by God Himself. You can then enter into His peace. "And He said to them, 'Go into all the world, and preach the gospel to every creature. He who believes and is baptized will be saved; but he that does not believe will be condemned. And these signs will follow those who believe; in My name they will cast out demons; they will speak with new tongues; they will take up serpents; and if they drink anything deadly, it will by no means hurt them; they will lay hands on the sick, and they shall recover'" (Mark 16:15–18).

"Great peace have those who love Your Law, And nothing causes them to stumble" (John 1:8). To find our peace and be able to walk in hope, we must know God's Word and what He accomplished at Calvary. We must keep His commandments. We must be able to distinguish good from evil and keep His precepts and testimonies.

God spoke to me, saying now is the time for His children to be healed mentally and physically, delivered from the spirit of unworthiness, from feelings of being unwanted and unloved to receive Him as our Shepherd. At the cross, an exchange took place for our perfect salvation plan with every provision made then set before us, if only we would believe and step out in faith. It was on the cross where Satan was defeated and his kingdom overthrown. It was at the cross that our salvation was made perfect and the problems of time was solved. "For God so loved the world that He gave His only begotten Son, that whosoever believes in Him should not perish but have everlasting life" (John 3:16).

Since the fall of Adam and Eve, the only hope for human race is the promise made by the prophet Isaiah: "Who has believed our report? And to whom is the arm of the Lord revealed? For he shall grow up as a tender plant, and as a root out of dry ground: he has no form nor comeliness; and when we shall see him, there is no beauty that we shall desire him" (Isaiah 53:1–2).

The Lord would lay on Jesus the iniquity of all humanity. He would be the atonement for all sin for those who would believe. The definition for *belief* is "to be of the opinion that something exists or is reality, especially when there is no absolute proof of its existence or reality or to be confident that somebody or something is good or will be effective." In other words, if we can believe that God's word is going to be effective over our life, then we can have what it tells us we have—a perfect salvation plan. All provisions are made possible; all our sins are removed because of our Savior on the cross. That exchange at the cross guarantees a full pardon of all sins, guilt, shame, and condemnation.

> In Him also we have obtained an inheritance, being predestinated according to the purpose of Him [meaning Christ] who works all things after the counsel of His own will [meaning it is made perfect]—a perfect salvation plan where nothing can be added nor taken away. (Ephesians 1:11)

A blood covenant was made (Isaiah 53:5). He was widely rejected (Isaiah 53:1, 2). He bore our sins and sorrow (Isaiah 53:4, 5). He was our substitute (Isaiah 53:6, 8). He voluntarily accepted our guilt and punishment, giving His life that we could live (Isaiah 53:4). He was oppressed and afflicted; He was bruised for our transgressions (Isaiah 53:5–7). Yet He opened not His mouth (Isaiah 53:7).

> He was taken from prison and from judgment
> For He was cut off from the land of the living;
> For the transgressions of My people He was stricken. (Isaiah 53:8)

Jesus did it all so we wouldn't have to live in bondage to the devil's power.

Leviticus 16:20 states, "And when he has made an end of reconciling the Holy Place, and the Tabernacle of the congregation, and the altar, he shall bring the goat. And Aaron shall lay both his hands upon the head of the live goat, and confess over him all the iniquities of the Children of Israel, and all their transgressions in all their sins, putting them upon the head of the goat."

Jesus took on Himself the very nature of a servant being made in human likeness, humbling Himself and becoming obedient to death so that you and I might be free from the power of death. The image of God taking His hand and laying it on the head of Jesus, transferring all sins of mankind upon the head of Jesus—this is the perfect sacrifice, the Lamb of God, the key for our salvation!

"Yet it pleased the Lord to bruise Him; He has put Him to grief; when you shall make His soul an offering for sin, He shall see His seed, He shall prolong His days, and the pleasure of the Lord shall prosper in his hand" (Isaiah 53:10). A shifting took place at the cross, and once we receive Jesus as Lordship over our life, His life for our death, we are reborn. Envision Jesus with our old book of record then taking His blood and dipping a cloth in the blood, wiping every page clean. We are now the seeds of God; no longer do we have to be concerned about the Adamic nature. We have been adopted, for our past no longer exists; it is under the blood of Jesus.

> I will be a Father to you, and you shall be My
> sons and daughters. (2 Corinthians 6:18)

> For as many as are led by the Spirit of God, these
> are sons of God. (Romans 8:14)

The Spirit Himself bears witness with our spirit that we are children of God and if children, then heirs, heirs of God, and joint heirs with Christ, if indeed we suffer with Him, that we may also be glorified together.

"What then shall we say to these things? If God is for us, who can be against us? He who did not spare His Own Son, but delivered Him up for us all, how shall He not with Him also freely give us all things" (Romans 8:31–32). Everything that belonged to Jesus belongs to me. I am a partaker of the blessings that God gave to Jesus.

"That the Gentiles should be fellow heirs, of the same body, and partakers of His promise in Christ Jesus through the gospel, of which I become a minister according to the gifts of the grace of God given to me by the effective working of His power" (Ephesians 6–7).

He gave to us the same Spirit, the same power and blessings, which is His anointing. We have the same authority in earth and the right to petition heaven for our needs by the Holy Spirit; He is our power. "But you shall receive power when the Holy Spirit has come upon you" (Acts 1:8).

"And Jesus came and spoke to them saying, all authority has been given to Me in heaven and earth. Go therefore and make disciples of all nations, baptizing them in the name of the Father and of the Son and of the Holy Spirit, teaching them to observe all things that I have commanded you; and lo, I am with you always, even to the end of days" (Matthew 28:18–20). Jesus left His disciples with a command to fulfill the Great Commission. It is through the Holy Spirit that we are equipped with His anointing and the power to accomplish this mission.

Jesus came so that He would fulfill prophecy, which was made complete at Calvary. He came so that we would be healed and sin would be removed far from us. "When the evening was come they brought Him [Jesus], many who were possessed with devils [demons]; And He cast out the spirit with His Word, and healed all who was sick. That it might be fulfilled which was spoken by the prophet

Isaiah, saying He Himself took on our infirmities and bore our sickness" (Matthew 8:16–17).

"He was wounded for our transgression and was bruised for our iniquities, the chastisement of our peace was upon Him; and with His stripes we are healed" (Isaiah 53:5). Jesus hung on the cross in agony and shame, forsaken by His disciples, rejected by His own people and heaven. With nothing left in this world, they took lots for His garments. Under supernatural darkness, with the uttering of the cry "It is finished," our salvation was made complete. God's Word never fails to accomplish His purpose.

"So shall My word be that goes forth out of My mouth; it shall not return unto Me void, but it shall accomplish that which I please, and it shall prosper" (Isaiah 55:11). The Hebrews viewed the spoken word as having a power of its own. Once it left the mouth of the speaker, it could never be recalled.

The result of our salvation could not have been achieved any other way than by the perfect sacrifice, the Lamb of God. His blood poured out as the atonement for our sins, a precious free "gift" from our Father God. Every sin that mankind will ever do is laid upon the head of Jesus so that we can be delivered from our sin and shame. We are indebted to Him and are now obligated to live according to God's statutes and concepts.

Colossians 2:15 tells how Jesus defeated Satan and his kingdom "having disarmed principalities and power, making a public spectacle of them, triumphing over them." In other words, Jesus pulled Satan through the streets, loudly announcing with great triumph that the victory was won. He offered up His soul for those who will believe by paying the price to redeem the whole human race.

In ancient times, if someone in Israel went bankrupt, they were to list all their debts on skin and post it for all to see. At times, a wealthy benefactor would come along and rescue and pay all their debts. He would take down the skin, double it over, and write his name on it, hence hiding all their debts. He would then post it as well so that all could come to him for payment.

"For your shame you shall have double honor, and instead of confusion, they shall rejoice in their portion: therefore in their land they shall possess the double; everlasting joy be upon you" (Isaiah 61:7).

When Jesus died on the cross, He atoned for all our sins. Upon faith in Him, He took down the list of our sins, doubled it over where they could no longer be seen, and wrote His name on the front, meaning that all our indebtedness was settled. Every single believer in the world has the privilege of possessing the "double" assurance that our sins are removed and no one will know. This is like a guarantee that our sins will never be remembered, never to be brought before us again. Jesus paid the indebtedness for all sins (Jimmy Swaggart Study Bible).

An exchange took place through the perfect sacrifice of Jesus on the cross. We will never live the fulfillment of peace and rest that was provided until we receive this perfect sacrifice. Jesus made it possible for us to enter into the secret place of His peace and rest, our secret place. Psalm 91:1 says, "He who dwells in the secret place of the Most High shall abide under the shadow of the Almighty."

Verse 8 says, "Only with Your eyes shall you behold and see the reward of the wicked." What God is saying here is "Come on in, pull up a seat, and see what is happening on the outside. Come into this place of rest."

The Father invited Jesus to come into this place through this same sacrifice that He invites you and me. Jesus was made sin with our sinfulness so that we might be made righteous with His righteousness. "In whom [Christ] we have redemption, through His Blood the forgiveness of sin according to the riches of His Grace" (Ephesians 1:7).

It is only through the Word that we learn of this knowledge of Christ on the cross and what it provided so that the eyes of our understanding can be enlightened to those truths. It is through God's Word that we receive the knowledge that enables the Holy Spirit to increase our vision of who we are through Christ and the cross and teaches us about our authority over the enemy. This is what Satan tries to keep us from learning and receiving.

God desires for us to come to this place of peace and rest. "Come unto Me, all you who labor and are heavy laden, and I will give you rest. Take My yoke upon you, and learn of me; for I am meek and lowly in heart: and ye shall find rest upon your souls. For My yoke is easy and My burden is light" (Matthew 11:28–30).

God is calling for us to be spiritually rooted deeper into the Spirit of God like never before. In the Spirit of God, there is a place that provides a constant source of divine life and Spirit of empowerment. There is a fountain that flows and never runs dry; it is the Holy Spirit of God.

"There is a river the streams make glad the city of God, the Holy Place of the Tabernacle of the Most High" (Psalm 46:4). The river is symbolic of the Holy Spirit, who alone brings life with Christ as its source and the cross as its means—in other words, abiding in Christ and knowing our identity. We must be assured of our identity through the price that Jesus paid at Calvary before we can enter into this river. We must know that in His blood, we are a new creation and accepted by God because He poured out His life for our life. "For with you is the fountain of life" (Psalm 36:9). He is waiting for us. He's waiting for us to experience what it is like to come into His presence simply for the joy and delight of being with Him for who He is, our "Bridegroom." He wants us to know this: "I am crucified with Christ nevertheless I live; yet not I, but Christ in me" (Galatians 2:20). Jesus is the life within us.

"He who is joined together to the Lord is One spirit in Him" (1 Corinthians 6:17). Nobody can separate us; it is sealed, and no one can change it. "It is finished."

To be able to see that the devil is defeated, we have to recognize he has lied to us about our identity, and to win our battle, we must crucify our thoughts, reframe our mind by binding it to the mind of Christ, and bind our will to the will of God. We must start thinking spiritually, seeing ourselves as God sees us—mighty saints of God. We are made in His image, in His likeness. We have spent most of our lifetime seeing ourselves as defeated, rejected, unwanted, unloved, and not worthy to walk in the call God has placed upon us. When we see ourselves any other way than what God sees, we are denying the blood, the Word of God. This is doubt and unbelief. We have to start believing. "I am who God's Word says I am! I am more than a conqueror. I am the head and not the tail." Jesus made it possible for us to be fully and totally justified at Calvary. We are now a new creation through His blood.

To enter this place of rest and peace, we need to take self-inventory of anything that doesn't line up with the Word of God and remove it far from us and envision the blood of Jesus flowing over us. That's what Jesus's blood did; it removed sin far from us and made us in the image of God. "Knowing this that our old man is crucified with Him [all that we were before Christ under His blood], that the body of sin might be destroyed [the power of sin broken] that henceforth we should not serve sin… Likewise reckon yourselves to be dead indeed unto sin, but alive through Christ our Lord" (Romans 6:6, 11). *Reckon* means to account or calculate something or to suppose something to be true; in other words, we are to take into account that what God's Word says is truth. We are in His image, in His likeness.

God the Father poured out His blood through His Son—His Son's life for our life—and no one can change this, for it is a finished work. Satan cannot undo what was accomplished at Calvary.

If we will seek God with all our heart, He will guide us to the ancient river that flows deep in the heart of our Father God. If you drink from this fountain, everything around you that is not from God will bow. "If we don't allow, they must bow." Your life will then change because of salvation, the price Jesus paid bringing this change. This change will unlock the door to the secret place, where He is calling us into. There we'll find God's unfailing love, and His love changes things. This is the door to our deep cleansing, mentally and physically. He desires our fellowship and waits for us to come into His presence, to enter into the King's chamber.

"Therefore if any man be in Christ, he is a new creation: old things are passed away; behold, all things are become new" (1 Corinthians 5:17). If we will surrender to Jesus and let Him live His life through us, we won't have near the battles to fight. Some of us are still trying to defeat Satan, when he is already defeated; Jesus did it all at Calvary.

We are the body of Christ and accepted into the house of the Beloved. "I will rejoice greatly in the Lord, my soul shall be joyful in my God; for He has clothed me with the garment of salvation, He has covered me with the robe of righteousness" (Isaiah 61:10). The technical word for this is *justified*. In other words, we have been tried in the supreme court of heaven, and the Judge has handed down the verdict: not guilty, saved by grace. There is now nothing the accuser can point his finger to accuse you with. It is finished; our salvation plan is made complete.

"For the wages of sin is death; but the Gifts of God is Eternal Life through Jesus Christ" (Romans 6:23). When Jesus was nailed to the cross, God transferred all the sins of humanity to the soul of Jesus. "For He has made Him to be sin for us, who knew no sin that we might be made the Righteousness of God Himself" (2 Corinthians 5:21). Jesus, through His love, poured out His life for us. The life of the flesh is found in the blood. Our Father's unfailing love giving us the blood of His Son, the soul of His Son given to us on the altar to make atonement for our sins. "For the life of the flesh is in the blood; and I have given it to you upon the altars to make atonement for your soul: for it is the blood that makes an atonement for the soul" (Leviticus 17:11).

He has poured out His soul unto death, meaning Christ not only died for man but poured out His soul with His own hand. He laid down His own life; no man took it. He did this for you and me! Jesus made our salvation complete. Imagine, as Jesus hung on the cross, hanging with Him was all the unworthiness and rejection Satan lied to us about. Jesus totally removed this from our existence. "Therefore we are buried with Him by baptism into death; that like as Christ was raised up from the dead by the Glory of the Father, even so we should walk in newness of life" (Romans 6:4).

We are the ones that allow ourselves to have so many battles because we don't see ourselves as who God tells us we are, the saints of God. If the voice you're listening to doesn't bring you joy and peace, it isn't God; this is giving place to the devil. Our victory comes through the Word of God. "Get thee behind me Satan," it is written. The Word says, "Commit and resist the devil and he will flee from you" (James 4:7). God's Word is our strength, our perfect weapon for our battles.

"The thief does not come except to steal, and kill, and destroy, I have come that they may have life, and have it more abundantly" (John 10:10). "Then Jesus said to them again, 'Most assuredly I say to you whoever comes before Me are thieves and robbers, but the sheep did not hear them, I am the door. If anyone enters by Me, he will be saved, and go in and out and find pastures'" (John 10:7–9).

The job of a shepherd is a tiring and dangerous one. Often the shepherd spends years with a particular herd of sheep and calls them by a descriptive name. As I read this, I thought, "What does this mean, a descriptive name?" Then the Holy Spirit quickened me and said, "Some had spots, some were black-faced, etc." I thought, "Oh." It's like when I look at someone, and they have a different nose, different eye color, and hair color. The Holy Spirit quickened me that we too are marked, marked by the blood of Jesus. This is how we are known by the Father. The sheep knew and followed the voice of the shepherd, but they would not respond to a stranger's voice. The shepherd went "before them" to make sure the path was safe for the sheep.

I am the good shepherd. The good shepherd gives His life for the sheep. But a hireling, he who is not a shepherd, one who does not own the sheep, sees the wolf coming and leaves the sheep and flees; and the wolf catches the sheep and scatters them. The hireling because he is a hireling does not care about the sheep. I am the good shepherd; and I know my sheep, and am known by My own. As the Father knows Me, even so know the Father, and I lay down My Life for the sheep. And other sheep I have which are not of the fold; them also I must bring, and they will hear My voice, and there will be one flock and one shepherd. (John 10:11–16)

A shepherd fed the sheep, led them to water. He guarded them; they left and wandered off and got lost. He protected them from predators (usually wolves). He carried them when they were sick or weak. He constantly cared for them. He gave His life for them. If this isn't a place to rest and walk in peace, there isn't any rest at all. Now is the time to read Psalm 23.

God said, "My Word is established in heaven." In other words, it cannot be changed. We are to establish it on earth, speak it, affirm it over our life, and let it become active over our life. I am who God's Word says I am! Proclaim your identity in Christ. Take your place in the kingdom.

> For we which have believed do enter into rest, as He said, As I have sworn in My wrath, if they shall enter into My rest: although the works were finished from the foundation of the world. For He (God) spoke in a certain place of the seventh day on this wise, And God did rest on the seventh day from all His works. Therefore giving us a place of rest. Seeing therefore it remains that some must enter therein, and they to whom it was first preached entered not in because of unbelief: Again, He limited a certain day, saying in David, Today, after so long a time; as it is said, Today if you will hear His Voice, harden not your hearts. For if Jesus had given them rest, then would He [God] not afterward have spoken of another day. There remains therefore a rest to the people of God. (Hebrews 4:2–9)

This place of rest that is talked about does not mean the land of Israel that Joshua led them into. If that were what God meant, He would not have spoken long afterward about "today" being the time to get in. So there is a full, complete rest waiting for the people of God. Christ has already entered there. He is resting from His works, just as God did after creation. Let us do our best to go into that place of rest, being careful not to disobey God as His children of Israel did, thus falling. Jesus finished what the law couldn't do; He provided the place of rest for God's people. We can now enter this rest through what Jesus did at Calvary because of the plan of salvation. Let us not be as the Israelites and not accept what Jesus has bought and paid the price for us to establish our journey to eternal life.

Our place of rest is in the throne room at the Father's right hand. "And has raised us up together, and made us sit together in heavenly places in Christ Jesus" (Ephesians 2:6).

Satan tried everything in his power to keep this from coming to past but failed. All the occult, all the witchcraft, all power of Satan have no power over our Almighty God if we give ear to what He is saying to us. "My son, give attention to My Words; incline your ear to My sayings. Do not let them depart from your eyes; keep them in the midst of your heart; for they are life to those who find them, and health to their flesh" (Proverbs 4:20–22). We must receive by faith Christ as our Lord and Savior and believe God's Word. Because of the cross, He has received us. He has adopted us into His family and assumed full responsibility for us; we belong to Him.

God didn't lie to David, and He'll not lie to us! The promises He made through Jesus Christ, we have them now if we will only believe and quit limiting God. God's Word is established through His spoken Word. We are to establish it in earth by His Word spoken over our life, letting it come alive and active over our life. We have eaten off the table of our enemy long enough; it is time to feast off the table of our Creator. Psalm 23:5 states, "You have prepared a table before me in the presence of my enemies. You have anointed my head with oil, my cup runneth over."

Satan has hidden our identity long enough. God wants us to see ourselves as He says we are: "The saints of God bought by the blood." For we are a new creation. We have allowed the struggle and pressure of the enemy to delude us, keeping us from seeing the completeness of our salvation. 2 Corinthians 1:2 states, "For I am jealous over you with Godly jealousy: For I have exposed you to one husband, that I may present you as a chaste virgin to Christ." (We must not commit spiritual adultery, which refers to trusting in things other than God's Word.) Anything that isn't God's Word is doubt and unbelief. It is the truth of God that we seek. He has proven His love for us by sending His Son to die in our place. Every provision was made for our past, present, and future at the cross.

"As for this is My Covenant with them, saith the Lord, My Spirit that is upon you, and My Word which I have put in your mouth, shall not depart out of your mouth, nor your seed, nor out of the mouth of your seeds seed, saith the Lord, from henceforth and for ever" (Isaiah 59:2). We are a new person, the seed of God. His blood poured out through His Son, Jesus Christ. He sent His Son to take back what Adam lost. God has taken away the old sinful nature and replaced it with the blood of His Son. We have been reborn.

Jesus said you can't put new wine into old skins. We can't be light and darkness. We can't serve two masters. Receive the cross and resurrection and let Jesus live His life through us. Know that we are no longer who Satan says we are but who God says we are; quit living the lie the devil has made us believe! "For as many are led by the Spirit of God they are the sons of God. For you have not received the spirit of bondage again to fear; but have received the Spirit of adoption, whereby we cry Abba, Father" (Romans 8:14– 15).

Jesus came from heaven to Earth. He walked through the earth to the cross and from the cross to the prison hell, from prison hell back to heaven. He came back through the person of the Holy Spirit. He came and poured out His soul for you and me. He stripped Satan of his power and authority over us so that we could have a place of rest and peace with our Father. The world tells us we are defeated, but we have overcome the world. "For whatsoever is born of God overcomes the world, even our Faith" (1 John 5:4). We are not of the world. We are only passing through. God's Word says that we are more than conquerors. Through salvation, we have a place of rest with God. All we have to do is believe and receive.

Paul made a noble statement in Acts 27:23. In the middle of a storm, he said, "For there stood by me this night the Angel of God, whom I am, whom I serve," the statement meaning "whose I am" and "whom I serve" and "whom I believe, God" (J. Swaggert). If we can envision this same free gift of salvation Paul received making the same confession, what can we accomplish?

We can reprogram our minds to the mind of Christ, for God speaks to us through His Word and through His Word by believing. "I am who God's Words says I am." "I have what God's Word says I have." We have to abide by His conditions to get there. We have to rise up and take our place in the kingdom, making the way for the coming of the Lord. We can do this only through commitment to fast and pray, by being a Joshua and building an altar before the Lord. He will reveal Himself to share the great salvation plan of total deliverance to liberty and freedom from all past sins. God saw us in the state of sin and sent down His love through His Son. It is through this act that we are made worthy and accepted into this place of perfect rest and peace.

It is time for us to rise up from depression and oppression and recognize the truth of God. "The truth will set you free." There is nothing about us that God doesn't already know, yet He still loves us. He knew us in our mother's womb. His Word says that before He sent Jesus, He knew us, He knew all the things we would do in my Adamic nature and He still sent His Son.

We must be free from all of Satan's lies about our not being worthy to receive God's gift of love and know that we have God's favor on us. We will live and not die and proclaim the works of the Lord. We are born of God and the evil one cannot touch us. We have to get our eyes off our failures and disappointments and turn our face back to God. We have to know that the only power the devil has over us is what we give to him. We have to know that God is for us. He loves us, for we are His possessions. There is nothing that Jesus did not secure for us in His perfect salvation plan. We have it all!

The spiritual realm is real—unseen but does exist. There is a spiritual war going on for your soul between God and Satan. This war is for the possession of your soul, mind, will, and emotions. It is very active and alive. Satan can make lies so real in our mind, and if we believe them, this is where the battle begins. These lies are a trap or snare that takes us captive. Satan gives us excuses and reasons to doubt who we are in Christ. Satan is a fallen angel who has become twisted on the inside, and he's trying to do the same to us with his lies, like one-third of the angels. The sooner we realize this and get revelation that we are being deceived, the sooner we can enter God's peace and win our battle. If we are going to be effective in winning the battle over our minds, we must realize the accuser comes to condemn. He whispers in the ear, building a stronghold on us and where a stronghold exists, it creates a demonically induced pattern of thinking. This becomes a dwelling place for satanic activity to enter and take root in your emotions.

One of Satan's main tools is creating the feeling of unworthiness, which makes us not see ourselves as God says we are. He loves to make us doubt God's Word and gives promises that will make us feel separated from God. He'll make us feel alone in the battle because our faith is pushed back and we can't receive. Then oppressions and depression takes place, building up fear and causing us to be anxious and worried and feel defeated so that we can't walk in our calling. It keeps us from hearing God's voice. Before we can claim victory, these strongholds must be pulled down to the mind of Christ, and what His Word tells us we is: "Repent, take your thoughts captive unto God casting down every lofty thing raised up against the knowledge of God" (2 Corinthians 10:5).

It is the truth of God's Word that establishes. We have to come to God and exchange our darkness for light. We have to receive these truths and receive a fresh new way of thinking and living, building and establishing our daily life on His foundation, building our house on the rock (Jesus), not the sand (devil).

It is through our lack of knowledge that Satan can keep us vain in our imaginations. He keeps our heart in darkness, where we can't see the light and know that Jesus accomplished all deliverance, all provision, our perfect Salvation at Calvary. "In whom also we have obtained, being predestined according to the purpose of Him"—this means Christ Jesus. "Who works all things after the counsel of His own will"—this means it is made perfect (Ephesians 1:11). If man doesn't learn the purpose of Calvary and Jesus and what He set in action and believe that God is the Creator of this universe and that He is who He says He is, we will never accomplish our destiny.

Our testing is in the knowledge of God's Word, knowing our purpose of Jesus on the cross. If Job had not known the Father's unfailing love, He would have failed his battle with Satan, but He knew God. He knew God's commandments and statutes. He knew the law of God, and he had kept them. Job's fear wasn't his battle; it was his knowing God's knowledge of him. This is why God allowed Job's battle; God knew he wouldn't fall. We must learn today to grow in the knowledge of Jesus Christ. Our test today is who we are because of the cross and resurrection. This is the reason for our battles; this is the victory over our battles. If Satan can keep our minds occupied on how unworthy we are and keep us feeling rejected and feeling like a failure, he wins. We have to remember, we are one with Christ.

"Submit yourselves therefore to God. Resist the devil, and he will flee from you" (James 4:7).

Our Salvation Plan

How many of us in our journey feel as if we've been battered and torn, that our boat is about to sink? God wants to let you know that we have been called, chosen, and sealed by the Holy Spirit. We are a new creation. God has given everyone a personal invitation to His salvation and His marriage supper.

"Ho, every one that thirsts, come to the waters, and he who has no money; come ye, buy, and eat; yea, come, buy wine and milk without money and without price" (Isaiah 55:1). I learned, in looking up the definition of *come*, that it means "to extend," "to arrive," "to appear as." Help will come; peace will come. It's time to come and get the meal.

Verse 2 says, "Wherefore do ye spend money for that which is not bread? and your labour for that which satisfieth not? hearken diligently unto me, and eat ye that which is good, and let your soul delight itself in fatness." I believe the *fatness* this verse speaks of is peace, prosperity, joy, and happiness that His salvation gives us. This is saying that accepting the Holy Spirit's invitation will satisfy your soul completely.

Isaiah 53 proclaims the great price that was paid for our salvation, which means deliverance. God will keep us. We are His vessels, His mouthpiece, and His feet. We are to deliver the message, fulfill the scriptures of this time and season. He is bidding us to come into the full purpose of the cross. We have to make that choice to come.

He is calling out a remnant of women in these last days. He is calling us to a place in Him, to be used totally by Him. He will stand with us and not let us down if we will only commit to Him. Like Paul said in 2 Timothy 4:17, "Notwithstanding the Lord stood with me, and strengthened me; that by me the preaching might be fully known." He will stand with us today too. His Word tells us that no one can take us out of His hand.

In the upper room, as they waited for the Holy Spirit, they were all in one accord. Today, God is calling us to be in one accord, one mind, and one body. As the body in Christ, we have to take our stand in Christ against our demons, together with one mind and one accord. He wants to put us in a position, and He needs us to be in one accord, having the same vision that God is trying to birth on earth. But first we have to be delivered, completely surrendered to God. See the same vision of God with one mind, one body, and know the true love our Father has provided for us. That is where your peace lies—in confidence and assurance of the Father's love. "For God so loved the world that He gave His only begotten Son, that whosoever believes in Him should not perish, but have Everlasting Life, but that the world through Him might be saved" (John 3:16–17). "Knowing this, that our old man is Crucified with Him [all that we were before conversion], that the body of sin might be destroyed that henceforth we should not serve sin" (Romans 6:6). Know that guilt, shame, and the power of the old nature of sin have been totally removed from our new life.

Jesus gave the command of His name to fulfill the Great Commission: "And these signs shall follow them who believe; In My name, shall they cast out devils; they shall speak with new tongues. They shall take up serpents; and drink any deadly thing, it shall not hurt them; they shall lay hands on the sick and they shall recover" (Mark 16:17). His name declares us master over Satan, giving us dominion over him and over all his works.

It is the finished work on the cross that we build our faith upon. "And He said unto them all if any man will come after Me let him deny himself, and take up his cross daily, and follow Me" (Matthew 16:24). What Jesus is saying here is, to deny your willpower, self-will, your strength and ability will depend totally upon Him. "Crucify your flesh." For a long time, I thought "Pick up my cross" meant I had to suffer each day of my life, but I finally realized that Jesus did the suffering for me. It took me a while to know He doesn't want me to suffer. He took all my suffering on Himself and is now sitting at the Father's right hand in heaven, where there is no suffering.

What these scriptures are saying is to pick up the benefits of the cross, to renew our faith and understand what Christ did for us at Calvary, and to apply it to our life on a daily basis. How can we be all God called us to be if we are lying in a bed of suffering? Through His Son's blood, we have been given a right standing in His kingdom.

We know that Satan will try to get our eyes off the cross, but we have to refuse to let the devil blind us. I realized that I allowed him to blind my vision long enough in so many areas of my life, even to the receiving of my benefits to the cross. He has a way of showing us our weaknesses and making us feel like a total failure. God has called us, and it is time for us to wake up and arise to the authority He has given. If only we would realize the full knowledge of the cross and the sanctification that has been provided us and submit ourselves to God. We have to keep our mind occupied on these benefits, writing them on the tablets of our heart, and know our legal rights that give us entrance into the throne room with no condemnation, no fear, and no guilt. Our peace is finding our place in the fullness of God's love.

"But if the Spirit of Him who raised up Jesus from the dead [Holy Spirit] dwell in you, He who raised up Christ from the dead shall also quicken your mortal bodies, will give us power in our mortal bodies that we might live a victorious life, by His Spirit who dwells in you" (Romans 8:11). We have that same Spirit in us that raised Jesus from the dead. That is why the devil is trying to keep our eyes off the cross and on our weaknesses.

Satan has had us in a battle for so long that we want to get in our house, shut the door, and never leave again. We've been in the battle so long that we can't find the way out. You feel like God has left you all alone. You've even become mad at God. We haven't realized it is His strength that we have been walking in, not our own. It is His strength that carries us, for our strength left us long ago in the battle. We are like the man with the footprints in the sand. It is not our footprints we see when we look back from where we came. "He gives strength to the weary, And to him who lacks might He increases power" (Isaiah 40:29).

We think we can't possibly let anyone know the battle we are in. "They will know I am facing demons," you say and then think you have sinned. Satan's voice has become so loud you can't hear our Master's soft, gentle voice that bids us to come to him, to not turn down that path: "Here I am. I'm over here!" All you can hear is "You've messed up this time. You will never be forgiven."

If only we can become conscious of the power and purpose of Jesus's shed blood on the cross and what we are about and the power we can walk in instead of what the devil can do to us or how weak and unworthy we are. If only we know that the blood of the Son of God at the cross is the price for our redemption and that the forgiveness of our sin is the remission of their penalty. This tells us that were we charged. We will be found not guilty. We have to know what His Word tells us. "Know you not, that so many of us are baptized unto Jesus Christ were baptized unto death? Therefore, we are buried with Him by baptism into His death that, like as Christ was raised up from the dead by the Glory of the Father, even so we also should walk in newness of life" (Romans 6:3–4). These scriptures tell me that I am now a new creation in Christ. He has now, after my repentance, taken Lordship over my life. He has brought us out of the slavery of sin and is now our Master. My old nature was crucified with Jesus. I am now walking in His nature, His likeness. We are now His righteousness, His sons and daughters, knowing that the new creation we received is the nature and life of God. "The Spirit itself bears witness with our spirit that we are the children of God" (Romans 8:16).

We have now been adopted into the house of the kingdom of God; we now have privileges because we are heirs. "Lo, children are an heritage of the Lord and the fruit of the womb is His reward" (Psalm 127:3). Since we are adopted, we have a legal right to what belongs to the Father, and I know this is true. I adopted my son, and after becoming mine, he has the legal right to what is mine.

This is the way it is with the Father. I never have to look back to where I came from. It doesn't matter what I did, what I was. I am now a new person, and my identity has been changed. I now carry my Father's name and now live in his kingdom. I belong to God. I am now royalty. I have the right to go before my Father and ask Him for what I need. I don't have to worry, for He will fight my battles. He loves me "after all." He gave His firstborn for me so that I could live and have all these things. All He owns is now mine. Romans 8:32 is my adoption papers, "He who spared not His own Son, but delivered Him up for us all, how shall He not with Him also freely give us all things?" Knowing this, we should be able to find peace that we've never had before. "Fear not little flock for it is your Father's good pleasure to give you the Kingdom" (Luke 12:32).

It is the cross that gave "all things" to us. No one can change this. It has already happened; it is finished. No one can separate me from my Father. Romans 8:38 tells me, "For I am persuaded, that neither death, nor life, nor angels, nor principalities, no power, nor things present, nor things to come, nor height, nor depth, nor creature, shall be able to separate us from the Love of God." This tells me that I never have to worry about my Father's love, for it was secured solely by the death of Jesus on the cross. It will never change, for it all happened at the cross. "I am in Christ Jesus." We are in the Father, sitting at the throne room.

There are so many scriptures that tell us who we are in Christ Jesus, but the greatest message is Jesus's death and resurrection. It is a finished work. Like I said, no one can change it. This is the covenant we have that binds Christ to the saints and the saints to Christ. We can now know we are the righteousness of God. We have to believe this and take our place in God. We have to believe the truths of His Word over the devil's lies. God's words are forever settled in heaven, and we have to establish them on earth—that is, to begin to apply them over our life. It is His Word we have to build our daily life upon. Once we accept His Word as truth and begin to build our life around His Word, we will become victorious. When we receive this and know who we are in Christ, all we have to do is open our mouth and let Satan know who we are. He already "knows." He wants to see if you know.

I believe his demons stand and laugh at us as they discuss the things they know that we "don't know." I believe they say, "If they only knew what authority they have in the name of Jesus, they would send us back to the dry places, but they're too busy praying at the altar for their sins to be forgiven and for their weaknesses. Don't they know Psalm 27: 1–2? 'The Lord is my Light and My Salvation; whom shall I fear?' They forget that they are the temple of the Living God, as God has said, 'I dwell in them, and I will be their God, and they shall be My people' [2 Corinthians 6:16]. They don't know they are the sanctuary of the Holy Spirit, all made possible by Calvary." When the wicked, even my enemies or my foes, came upon me to eat up my flesh, they stumbled and fell. It is sad when our enemy knows who we are in Christ but we do not.

In the Old Testament, God brought His people out of bondage through Moses. How much greater is God's promise for His people in the New Testament for our deliverance because of Calvary? We have the greater weapon—the name and the blood of Jesus. Satan could never compete with His name or His blood.

Our minds have to be renewed in the truths of God's Word daily. We must have a clear vision of our benefits of the cross and of our redemption, knowing that Christ carried His blood into the holy of holies and sprinkled it on the mercy seat. He made the purification for our redemption. "Who delivers us out of the authority of darkness and Thine, and Thine are Mine, and I am glorified in them and now I am no more in the world, but these are in the world, and I come to You, Holy Father, keep through Your Own Name those whom You have given to Me, that they may be one, as we are." (1 Colossians 1:13; John 17:21)

God is calling us out of the control of the world and its system, out of the control of Satan's lies. God is calling us to Himself, to commit to Him in one accord, one mind, and one body. He desires to put His people in unity with Him and each other. But we have to know who we are in Christ Jesus. We have to know the price that was paid at Calvary. We have to receive the greatest message of the cross and resurrection, and that is to know the power and authority it gives us. It takes faith to believe the report of Jesus's finished work on the cross. We are now partakers of the divine nature.

We have to come out of the slavery of sin consciousness and not be dominated by the devil's lies. We have to know that Jesus is our salvation and begin to see ourselves worthy of the Lamb's blood that was shed at Calvary. We need to know that no one can bring charges against us for our past, for when we go before the Father, He doesn't see us but sees the spotless Lamb that was provided for us, just like He provided for Abraham. No longer does Satan own me, because the sacrifice was given through the Lamb, which was provided for me. I now belong to a heavenly kingdom, and my sins have been atoned for.

When God told Abraham that Sarah was going to give birth, even though he knew their bodies were dead, Abraham didn't doubt. He refused to look at the condition of their bodies and waited for it to come to pass. Abraham was the descendant for his time and season as Jesus is for our time and season.

There is nothing in the world that can rule me—no sickness, no lack—for I am free from the curse and from bondage. "Now the God of peace, that brought again from the dead our Lord Jesus Christ, that great shepherd of the sheep, through the blood of the everlasting covenant. Make you perfect in every good work to do His will, working in you that which is well pleasing in His sight, through Jesus Christ; to whom be glory forever and ever Amen" (Hebrews 13:20–21). Jesus is the foundation we have to build our faith upon.

It was my sin that Jesus carried to the cross. For my sicknesses and diseases, He went to the whipping post, and when we speak of our weaknesses, we are manifesting them. What we say we have is what we have. "Death and life are in the power of the tongue: they that love it shall eat the fruit thereof" (Proverbs 18:21). If you plant the seed, this translates you unto the kingdom of His dear Son, "in whom we have redemption, through His blood, even the forgiveness of sin" (Colossians 1:14).

"For then must He often have suffered since the foundation of the world: but now appeared to put away all sin by the sacrifice of Himself" (Hebrews 9:26). The sacrifice Jesus made for us had only to be made one time. It removed all our sins; not one sin remains.

I want you to do something. I want you to close your eyes and see Jesus hanging on the cross. He is beaten, has nails in his feet and hands. He is wearing a crown of thorns; His side is torn, and His blood flows down to the ground. Now say, "My sin did this." Now do you see how any sin from our past could be carried over to this new creation?

We have lost our identity, who we are, because of Calvary. We have to return to our first love, Jesus on the cross. I truly believe we have taken our eyes off Calvary. How many times do you hear the word Calvary spoken today? Jesus gave us perfect fellowship with God. As we stand before our Father, He no longer sees our sin but His Son's blood. The cross and resurrection makes us masters over our enemies, over the darkness, over the evil world.

I'm telling you, it is up to you if the journey you are traveling is smooth or rocky by believing and receiving God's Word, applying it over our circumstances, and speaking it out of your mouth. God's Word is creative power. It will not return null or void. It can also determine how long you will stay in your battle. It is the difference between life and death.

God declares our righteousness through Jesus crucified on the cross. "For if we have been planted together in the likeness of His Death, we shall be also in the likeness of His Resurrection" (Romans 6:5). This should let us know we should be walking in the supernatural and not the natural; that we are in the world but not of the world.

The moment we make Him Lord over our life, we become His representatives in the earth. We can act in the authority of His Name. In this new creation, we are branches of the vine, members of His body. He is the vine; we are the branches.

We can now have clear vision of John 17:9–11: "I pray for them: I pray not for the world, but for them which you have given to me; for they are Thine and all Mine are yours." You will have the harvest, so learn the Word of God and speak healing and health over your life. "For other foundation can no man lay than that which is laid, which is Jesus Christ" (1 Corinthians 3:11). This is the foundation we build our life upon.

We have got to make the decision to rise up above the devils lies and deceit, rise up to God's calling and "seek ye first the Kingdom of God and His Righteousness" and activate our life according to His Word. The more we seek Him, the more we'll find Him.

God has given us a precious gift, His son's life on the cross, which renewed us as Spirit filled and walking in the Spirit in full communion with God. This is where we should find our peace. "And ye are Christ's; and Christ is God's" (1 Corinthians 3:23). All we need is in our Father's house.

"What? Do you not know that your body is the Temple of the Holy Ghost which is in you, which you have of God, and you are not your own?" (1 Corinthians 6:19). God is calling us to rise into the unity of the Godhead as one, walk in unity with each other as one; only then can He use us. We have to make a step toward Him in confidence and in assurance that we are His. Our mind has to be totally persuaded that we are a new creation through the cross, which brings the evidence of a newness of life.

Our past sins are buried in the tomb. We have to know who we are in Christ and know we are delivered from Satan's dominion. We are a light set on a hill to heal the brokenhearted, to heal the sick, to set the captive free. All the work Christ did, we can do. "Verily, verily, I say unto you, He that believeth on Me, the works that I do shall he do; because I go to the Father" (John 14:12). God desires to use us in the greater works.

What draws the sinner is the anointing of the Holy Spirit. He is the One that convicts sins. God wants to birth some things into existence; He is picking a remnant of women in these last days to give birth. But we have to know this: "I am crucified with Christ. Nevertheless I live—not I, but Christ lives in me. And the life that I now live in the flesh, I live by faith of the Son of God, who loves me and gave Himself for me."

Most of our battles are brought on because of disobedience. Remember what it did in the Garden of Eden? It brought spiritual death to Adam and Eve. If we didn't do what God told us to do and let the devil put us in fear, don't you think it will do the same for us today? How can we grow spiritually if we let the devil come and steal our visions? We have to go back where we last heard His voice and do what He said to do. We have to remember our steps are ordered by the Lord, and say, "Father, I'm stepping out in faith and believing that You will meet me there."

Think about Mary. She had no relationship with any man. It was the Holy Spirit that impregnated her. Look at whom she birthed: our Redeemer, our Savior, our Salvation, the Messiah—Jesus. Jesus was conceived through the Holy Spirit. Now we receive the same Holy Spirit that the Lamb provided for us. We are members of His body, His flesh, and His bones. We are joint heirs of the kingdom of God. We are now one in Jesus and one in the Father. The same Spirit of the Godhead resides in us. Our lives will change when we begin to walk in the greater works that He said we could.

When we begin to apply the Word over our trials and take our place as ambassadors of Jesus, in the Father's righteousness, we will triumph over the principalities of darkness and out of the battles of our mind and know we have the mind of Christ. We will then begin to realize that we can do all things through Christ Jesus, who strengths us. We shall lay our hands on the sick, and they shall recover. The demons are subject to the authority and power of Jesus through us.

You will discover we are sinners saved by grace, that we are not filthy rags. You will know that we are sinners saved by grace and have been washed in the blood of the Lamb. We are the righteousness of God! We have to line our life up with the Word of God and walk in the truth of His Word. Then we can rise up to where God has called us. We will rise up in those truths and take authority over our demons through the power of the Holy Ghost; walk in His supernatural. We can now speak peace, be still over the power of the storms trying to overpower our walk. Know that we have been delivered over to the hands of the Father because He gave His Son.

As long as we allow Satan to deceive us about our legal right, about our authority over him, about our dominion over the earth, we are denying the power of the Holy Ghost and the power of the blood that was shed on the cross. We are saying what Jesus did for us wasn't good enough, and we're denying the full effect of His blood. It will keep you from knowing that you belong to a heavenly kingdom, a divine nature.

We have to get hold of the reality of the indwelling of the Holy Spirit of God. We need to rise up and know the voice that taunts our mind with untruths about ourselves and know he is trying to destroy our mind and take our vision. We need to demand in the name of Jesus, "Get behind me, Satan! For it is written, let us not hear the voice that charges you."

We cannot compromise our legal right to enter into our Father's house. We need to take possession of what the devil doesn't want us to have, what rightfully belongs to us. We have to be renewed in our minds to the truths of God. We are valuable to God. Satan fights us because he knows who equips us. We are equipped with the Godhead, the Trinity of God the Father, the Son, and the Holy Ghost.

We have to take the Word of God and knock the devil out in the first match. What if we fast with the scripture over our circumstance for forty days? Can you imagine what would happen in our spirit realm? He wants to put us in a place where we've never walked before. I'm telling you, something in the spirit realm is about to happen! We can be a part of this move of God if we come when He calls. We are the righteousness of God, and He will perfect that which concerns us.

We have to take the authority God has given us and walk in it. We need to fix our eyes on the cross, go back to Calvary, and get back on the path of His righteousness. We need to be delivered from our flesh, jealousy, envy, strife, unforgiveness, and gossip. When we manifest the power of God on earth, we will see people get up out of the tomb and out of their grave clothes.

Before we can triumph over our battles, we must know that Satan has no power left; Jesus has defeated him. We are subject to God and escape from the snares of the devil. We have been called into a kingdom. "Wherefore seeing we also are compassed about with so great a witness, let us lay aside every weight, and sin which does so easily beset us. And let us run with patience the race that set before us" (Hebrews 12:1–2). Don't let the devil or anyone take your eyes off Jesus no matter what. But know who His Word says we are—His righteousness.

Now we have the scriptures to prove who we are, a new creation. We have rebirth through Christ Jesus. We have been adopted and have dominion over our enemy. Now we can take our place with God, in the Godhead. We no longer have to deny the power or the blood. We can begin to answer the call upon our life and walk in our gifts to live a victorious life.

We have received the truths of God and can become mighty warriors against Satan and his demons and win the battle. We now know this: "The Spirit of the Living God is upon me! He has anointed me to preach the good tidings unto the meek; He hath sent me to bind up the broken hearted, to proclaim liberty to the captive, and the opening of the prison to them that are bound. To proclaim the acceptable year of the Lord, and the day of vengeance of our God; to comfort all that mourn" (Isaiah 6:1).

I'm not saying that it is going to be like putting icing on a cake. The devil is real, and it is his job to steal, kill, and destroy. But know this: "If you were of the world, the world would love his own: but because you are not of the world, but I have chosen you out of the world, therefore the world hates you" (John 15:19).

"These things I have spoken to you, that in Me you might have peace. In the world you shall have tribulation: but be of good cheer, I have overcome the world" (John 16:33). He says He overcame the world so we can rest in total confidence, knowing we are under His control and covering. How can we lose? We have to recognize our demons, call them by name, and cast them out, crucifying our flesh and becoming the person God has called us to be.

His Word tells us that in the world, there is destruction, but we are not of the world. We must speak His Word into existence in our life. By speaking negative things over ourselves and others, we are speaking words of the enemy, and those words will hold us in bondage. Affirming God's Word over ourselves is crucial because it speaks life into our spirit, body, and soul. In Ephesians 6, we are instructed to take the sword of the Spirit and pray at all times. We apply the

Word personally over our live daily, not adding to or taking away from it, in the name of Jesus. The power lies in God's Word.

God's Word is our anchor; it is our lifejacket when we are in the storms of life. We have to form our world into existence by speaking God's Word over our circumstances. His Word is His voice spoken over our life. "But thou, Lord, art most high for evermore. For, lo, thine enemies, O Lord, for, lo, thine enemies shall perish; all the works of iniquity shall be scattered. But my horn shalt though exalt like the horn of an unicorn: I shall be anointed with fresh oil. Mine eyes also shall see my desires on mine enemies, and mine ears shall hear my desire of the wicked that rise up against me. The righteous shall flourish like the palm tree; he shall grow like the cedar of Lebanon. Those that be planted in the house of the Lord shall flourish in the courts of our God. They shall still bring forth fruit in old age; they shall be fat and flourishing" (Psalm 92:1–14).

We don't just speak His Word; we have to believe it is truth! Faith comes more quickly when you hear yourself quoting, speaking, and saying things God said. You will more readily receive God's Word into your spirit by hearing yourself speaking it out loud every day than if you hear someone else say it. We have an inner ear to our soul, and that is how we can receive—by hearing ourselves speak it aloud. Hearing ourselves speak the Word of God out loud every day for thirty days will change our life. "So then faith comes by hearing and hearing by the Word of God" (Romans 10:17).

Proverbs 18:21 states, "Death and life are in the power of the tongue." In the Amplified Bible, this is "The tongue can kill or nourish life." Words are powerful, but God's Word is full of creative power. Speaking His Word over your circumstance can line up your life with His Will for your life. We have to lose our will and bind together with His will.

These are the last days He is picking a remnant of women. He wants to take possession of some areas of our life. We won't know until the deemed time what we are to do. For the ladies that walk in His will, changes will be seen in our lives. He wants to give us "Beauty for ashes, the oil of joy for mourning, the garment of praise for the spirit of heaviness" (Isaiah 61:3). For I'm telling you, God is calling us out. He wants to raise us up, awaken us to His last call, and put us in unity as sisters in Christ.

I'm not being ugly, but I am going to tell you what God has given me for this body of Christ in this time and season. I sure don't want to put anyone into condemnation, but there is a lost and dying world outside of the church and our homes. We are going to be held responsible for how we have spent our time. All He wants is for us to make Him our first love. If we do that, I believe He will make it easy for our second love—our family and friends. I believe this will allow us to be able to stop fighting time. He will make sure we have time for our family, and we won't be as tired as we are now. We have all been called into the same ministry Jesus was called into, to heal the sick and set the captive free.

In Luke, a scripture reads, "Pressed down, shaking, running together, give and it shall be given unto you." I firmly believe this scripture has more than just one meaning. I believe it also means we are to give the Word of God, the love of God, and then our needs will be met in abundance.

> Is it time for you, O ye, to dwell in your pan-
> eled house, and this house lie in waste? [He is
> speaking of the house of God.] Now therefore
> thus said the Lord of hosts; Consider your ways.
> Ye have sown much, and bring in little; ye eat,
> but ye have not enough; ye drink, but ye are not
> filled with drink; ye clothe you, but there is none
> warm; and he that earneth wages earneth wages
> to put in a bag with holes. Thus saith the Lord of
> hosts; Consider your ways. Go up to the moun-
> tain, and bring wood, and build the house; and
> I will take pleasure in it, and I will be glorified,
> saith the Lord. (Haggai 1:4–9)

It is time to build God's house. Psalm 127:1 says, "Except the Lord build the house, they labour in vain who build it; except the Lord keep the city, the watchman waketh but in vain."

We are in the last days, and it is time for us to be totally committed to God and be in unity with one another. We need to help build each other up in faith. We need to get along with each other. As humans, we are going to make mistakes, so we need to not condemn one another but help each other get through what is going on.

We have got to begin walking in faith and not by sight. Hebrews 11:6 states, "But without faith, it is impossible to please God: for he that cometh to God must believe that He is, and that He is a rewarder of them that diligently seek Him." This is our word from God that He wants us to hear. By taking the word that He has given and receiving it, this will bring the abundance, rest, peace, and presence of God in our life that we have been searching for.

God is picking a remnant of women to rise up to His call, but we must not take this call lightly. We are to heed His call and be dressed and ready to move in the areas He wants to take us. There are unseen hands waiting to take us in His arms and lead us to a place we've never been before.

He wants to birth His love, His Holiness within us, but first we have to be delivered from the demons of envy, jealousy, gossiping, and unforgiveness. I'm telling you, this blood will turn the storm in your life back in Satan's face! We are the ones that have to make the commitment. We are the ones that have to know who we are in Christ.

> The Lord is my Light and my Salvation; whom shall I fear? the Lord is the strength of my life; of whom shall I be afraid? When the wicked, even my enemies and my foes, came upon me to eat up my flesh they stumbled and fell. Though an host should encamp against me, my heart shall not fear, though war should rise against me, in this will I be confident. One thing have I desired of the Lord, that will I seek; that I may dwell in the House of the Lord all the days of my life, to behold the beauty of the Lord, and to enquire in His temple. For in time of trouble He shall

hide me in His pavilion: in secret of His tabernacle shall He hide me; He shall set me up upon a
rock. (Psalm 27:1–5)

Oh come, let us worship and bow down; let us
kneel before the Lord our maker. For He is our
God; and we are the people of His pasture, and
the sheep of His hand. Today if you will hear his
voice. (Psalm 95:6–7)

Then you will call upon me and go and pray to
me, and I will listen to you. And You will seek
me and find Me, when you search for me with all
your heart. (Jeremiah 29:12–13)

One Night with the King

Time is getting short. With each tick of the clock, our lives are passing us by. Our journey on earth is coming to an end. The only way we will escape death is through the blood that Jesus shed on the cross. "I am Alpha and Omega, the beginning and the end, saith the Lord, which is to come" (Revelation 1:8). Did you know God works the night shift? One night with the King can change our lives.

We live in a world of wickedness. Most people have no fear of God; they don't even recognize Him as God anymore. The Bible tells us that in the last days, there will be scoffers who will laugh at the truth and say, "Where is your God?" Before I became a Christian, I remember someone telling me Jesus was coming and I said, "I've heard that all my life." We need to be prepared, for I tell you this day: "Jesus *is* coming soon!"

Satan tries to put us in the fire when we are tired and tempted. We need to be like Shadrach, Meshach, and Abednego and know that God, whom we serve, is able to deliver us from the fiery furnace. And we will come out of the furnace without even the smell of smoke upon us. "Blessed is a man who perseveres under trial for once he has been approved, he will receive the crown of life; which the Lord has promised to those who love Him" (James 1:12).

Jesus is calling us to intimacy, to draw closer to Him, to get ready for his coming. His door is always open. How willing are we to make the sacrifice of laying down our flesh and picking up the cross? It will come only through commitment to Christ, receiving Him as our Savior, for He is our Redeemer. *Redeemed* means purchased from slavery to freedom or nonownership, kinsmen-redeemer. He redeemed us with His blood. Do you see why the devil hates us? Every time he looks at us, he sees Jesus's blood. Jesus paid the ransom for us. Now let me tell you what *ransom* means: payment money, redemption money, purchased from slavery to freedom or new ownership; by extension, divine salvation from oppression; death or sin redeemed.

Jesus longs to have fellowship with us. His heart is full of hidden treasures He wants to share with us, but we have to be willing to make the sacrifice within our flesh. We have to be fashioned in his image. He came to establish the kingdom of God. Giving lordship over life, He established authority over our enemies. His blood covers a multitude of sins. It is the blood of Jesus that conquers all things. Therefore, the giving of His blood washed us white as snow, giving us new life. *New* means "to appearing, through of, developed, discovered, made for the first time, recently grown; fresh, Modem, recent, fashionable, having just reached a position rank, place, as a new arrival refreshed in spirit, health as men" (*Strong's Concordance*).

This tells me that there is no sin from our past lives that can be carried over into our new life with God. The only thing from our past that can interfere is the lies from Satan, the father of lies. No matter what our circumstance, God will deliver us out of our afflictions and give us wisdom, just like He delivered Joseph and gave him wisdom in the sight of Pharaoh. These are trying times. I would not want to be without Him.

God has a plan; no longer does the old spirit of wickedness live in us, for we are free. We must not forget who has given this eternal life to us. We must always go to Him with our praise and thanksgiving. "Then beware lest you forget the Lord who brought you out of the land of Egypt, from the house of bondage" (Deuteronomy 6:12).

The book of Deuteronomy is a powerful book written by Moses prior to the nations of Israel entering the land of Canaan. Moses knew he would not go with them; his death was imminent. Therefore, Moses used this to make the laws and commandments of God clear to the people.

Moses was calling upon the people of Israel to remember their God. Much faith had been required of the leaders. The years had worn down the people. After forty years in the wilderness, they could then see their reward. It was time to praise God for their deliverance. Much faith is also required of us today. We too have a reward if we stay on the path of righteousness. Many years have passed in our journey, many trials, but let us not forget who paid the ultimate price.

How many times do we ask God for something, only to finally receive it and never thank Him for the gift? The answers He supplies are life changing. He deserves our praise. Our praise is not just to take place in the church. What if God only supplied your needs in church? No! God's goodness deserves to be shouted from the mountaintops. After all, many times He meets us in our valleys.

We must surrender to Him, forsaking all flesh and worldly ways to dwell in the holy of holies, having a willing heart to abandon everything in order to yield itself to the authority and power of the blood of Jesus. We must be willing to pay the price He requires of us for this new beginning He has chosen for us. That is the only way we will be able to go beyond the veil—by the tearing of our flesh, nailing our flesh to the cross, and renting our hearts.

I know that some will not desire to do this because it hurts having our flesh pierced. The Father desires us totally for Himself. He gave a gift that not one of us could have given—His Son's blood, which assures us full pardon from death. There was a price to be paid for sin. Jesus paid that price.

We never have to ask Jesus "Do you love me?" as we do our spouses from time to time. He proved it on the cross. Do not let the devil keep you in shame or condemnation. "There is therefore now no condemnation to them which are in Christ Jesus, who walk not after the flesh, but after the Spirit" (Romans 8:1). You have been given a new life, having made peace through the blood of the Lamb on the cross.

In Psalm 18, David said, "In my distress I called upon the Lord, and cried unto my God; he heard my voice out of his temple, my cry came before him, *even* into his ears. Then the earth shook and trembled; the foundation also of the hills moved and were shaken, because he was wroth." In this chapter, there are fifty verses telling how God came to David's defense. David said, "He gave me the necks of my enemies." He will do the same for you and me. But we have to pray blessings and not cursing over our enemies.

Jesus endured all things so that the saints of God can obtain salvation, which is in Him. He also gave us the Holy Spirit as a guarantee of the fulfillment of His promises. We can be confident knowing He perfects that which concerns us. The Holy Spirit, which is God's Spirit in us, guides saints into all truths. He brings victory over our flesh by imparting faith; He is the one that imparts the gifts. The Holy Spirit baptizes the believers in Christ and convicts us of sin.

I believe now is the time He is calling the sinner to repentance. He's calling the lukewarm to wake up, the sinner to salvation, and the backsliders home. For this you know that no fornicator or unclean person or covetous man who is an idolater has any inheritance in the kingdom of God. "For to be carnal minded is death; but to be spiritually minded is life and peace. Because the carnal mind is enmity against God, for it is not subject to the law of God neither indeed can be" (Romans 8:6–7).

"The Spirit itself bears witness with our spirit that we are children of God. And if children then heirs; heirs of God, and joint-heirs with Christ; if so be that we suffer with *him*, that we may be also glorified together" (Romans 8:16–17).

God has been waiting for you. The veil was torn and the blood sprinkled. There is now no curtain; it was torn from the top to the bottom the day of the cross. Jesus is the curtain between us and God. We can now enter God's presence anytime. He longs to hear our praises. Our praises can change our life and will give us His peace and ease of rest.

Our life on earth will come to an end. All the parting will be over. As we grow older, what have we accomplished? There is nothing to gain in this earth; to gain it all and lose your soul is worth nothing, for there is coming a judgment day. Our life on earth will someday end, and if the rapture hasn't taken place, we will die. Our life on earth is but a destiny. As time passes when our destiny is over, it will be as though you never existed, never walked through this life, so what did you accomplish?

The only way we can accomplish anything that will bring rewards, any crowns after death is to let Jesus be the foundation we build on, leaving the gift of eternal life to our children, grandchildren, and friends. Jesus is the only way we can accomplish anything with purpose.

Any life without Jesus is death, and once the door to death is closed, there is no reopening. It is forever! If we live in sin, we are still dead; but if we live in the Spirit of God, we live even after death. Let us be a seeker of God's heart, wanting Him for our Master. If God is the life giver, I want Him for my God.

All through the generations, God has appointed men. He set them in place for the time and season to fulfill the scripture. We are appointed in this time and season to fulfill the scripture for the soon coming Messiah.

Moses was one of the chosen men in the Old Testament. God chose him to bring his people out of Egypt. Moses didn't think he was the man to do this because of his speech impediment, so God sent him a helper. He sent Moses a voice through Aaron. Aaron was to Moses what the Holy Spirit is to us. No matter what our mission, the Holy Spirit is our teacher. We have the Word for this time and season.

As I was studying my lesson about how God spoke to Abraham and told him to take Isaac to Mount Mariah, the Holy Spirit talked to me about how it was Abraham's faith that made him obey what God ordered. It was God's promises that moved Abraham. It was his faith in God's Word. Abraham knew that a blood covenant had been made. It was these promises that led him to the top of the mountain. He had faith that God would provide the lamb or, if need be, raise Isaac from the dead. God had told him that it would be through Isaac that his offspring would be reckoned.

God said to me, "If I was Abraham's God, am I not your God? Will I not keep the promises I made through my Son's blood?" Jesus made the provision for us. He paid the ransom. Can we have the faith, knowing the price has already been paid? The Father has provided the Lamb for us—Christ Jesus, our Redeemer.

When Moses brought the people out of Egypt, there was a demon walking among them whispering in their ear, causing confusion, doubt, and division as he does for us today. The demon persuaded Aaron to mold a false god for them, the golden calf (Exodus 32:4). Moses came down just before Satan consumed them. That's the way Jesus is when we are in a battle that we think we want win. He will come.

I believe we have been called at this time and season. God wants us to arise, stand firm without wavering or fainting, and know the Lamb has been provided for us. Each one of us has been given gifts for this time and season, so we need to commit totally. When He calls, we have to go. It will take each one of our gifts working together in unity for the last day of harvest. If we think a few have only been chosen, we will miss out on what He has fashioned us for.

"Now there are diversities of Gifts, but the same Spirit. And these are different of administration, but the same Lord. And there are diversities of operations, but it is the same God, which works all in all. But the manifestation of the Spirit is given to every man to profit withal" (1 Corinthians 12:4–7). The gifts are so important to the fulfillment of God's work that Jesus dedicated time while here on the earth to explain their place and use and many are for the edifying of the church (read 1 Corinthians 12, 14).

The gifts of wisdom, knowledge, healing, working of miracles, prophecy, discernment, divers kinds of tongues, and interpretation of tongues are all given through the same Spirit, which divides to every man at His will. He strategically placed every member of the body as it pleased Him so there would be no division. The members are to have the same mind, one for the other. If one member suffers, all suffer with him. If one is honored, all rejoice with him. We are to let God know that we desire the best gifts and He will be faithful to show you a more excellent way to use the gift and its design. Know that the presence of God carries His voice and the gift carries yours.

Let us arise from demons that assault us and stand like the cedars of Lebanon, firmly rooted and grounded in His word, knowing we have been sealed with the Holy Ghost. No matter what we try to take pleasure in, whether it is money, alcohol, or drugs, we will not find peace in the world. Sooner or later, it will overpower us. We belong to God. He is our creator and calls us to His will. Our purpose as a born-again believer is to finish God's work here on earth.

We tend to get too comfortable and become content where we are. God has given us a mission as He did with Abraham and Moses. We should start our day with the question "What can I do today for you, Lord? Take me where you need me to go." Without asking God what he would have us to do, we open the door for trouble. When the aggravation begins, we make the statement "This has been the worst day of my life." Or we end up being somewhere we didn't intend to be, and we have wasted our whole day. The only way we can have a successful life is letting God be in control, letting His Word become alive and active in our body, letting it be Jesus living in us as an embryo that forms life and gives life through birth. Let His life be birthed through us, putting on His righteousness and crucifying our flesh. Only then can we reflect the glory of the Lord as Moses did. In Christ, there is coming a resurrection.

If a man is in Christ, he is a new creature. Old things have passed away. Behold all things on earth or things in heaven. All things have been made new. Our sins have been done away with. We were adopted into the house of the saints through Jesus's shed blood. I know I keep repeating this, but we have to see it. I ask God when I look at myself to let me see myself covered in the blood of the Lamb that He provided.

It is a fact that God loves us. His love is true and never changing, never ending. Now is the time to prove how much we love Him, by laying down our life for Him. He has kept His covenant for thousands of generations because He has plans for us. He is calling us to rise up and take the place that He created for us.

As I lay in my bed early one morning, listening to the morning traffic, I was thinking about Jesus and wondering why he rose early to go before God. I realized the words "God is life" have more meaning than we can ever know. God has more power than we can comprehend. His Word creates life. I believe that God stands as the morning light, emerging after His creation has laid in slumber, His power coming forth. I believe He is at His full attention, watching as

His creation opens up its bosom, bringing forth the morning birth. The life He gives ushers in peace, joy, love, happiness, assurance, and rest. His light will break the yoke of darkness. "Then spake Jesus again unto them, saying, 'I am the Light of the world, he that followeth me shall not walk in darkness, but shall have the light of life'" (John 8:12).

You are not your own but are His property now. We are his! What freedom that brings to us. I believe that puts up a No Trespassing sign to the enemy. "Bring on the victory! Bring on the deliverance!" When we worship Him in truth and Spirit, our enemy will flee. Let us not become as the Jews when they turned their rebellious and stubborn shoulders and made heavy their ears. They made their hearts as stone or diamond points. He turned His ears from their cries. He scattered them.

There is no greater weapon than His Word. Do not let yourself be dragged down under the enemy's feet. All men are exalted to praise God. "Make a joyful noise unto the Lord, and come before His presence with joyful singing, entering unto His gates with thanksgiving and His courts with praise" (Psalm 100). He loves worship. If you want your prayers answered, praise Him! When we praise Him, the heavens bow down before Him and tremble.

The Egyptians were called out to serve Him; we are called out to worship (Isaiah 6:1–3). The seraphim sang, "Holy, holy, holy is the Lord of Hosts. The whole earth is filled with the glory of the Lord." The temple's foundation began to shake, and the sanctuary filled with smoke. If we could see the scars He carries for our salvation, I believe the whole earth would shake today from our praises. One of the seraphims flew and picked up a coal and touched Isaiah's lips as he began to see his faults. He said, "Your sins are forgiven." That is what the blood of Jesus does for us; it tells us that our sins have been forgiven.

We are prepared beforehand for what God has called us to, so when Satan tries to take your peace and confidence, remind him of what he already knows—the same Nazarene you serve is the same one that carried your cross. God is your Master, and Satan knows he has no power over you. He tries to make you think he does.

When someone leaves you something in their will, that means you become owner of that property. That's what the blood of Jesus did for you; what every Word of God says belongs to us. It is ours! When Jesus died, he left us heirs of God. That means anything the devil tries to take from you is illegal. He's stealing from you, and he has no authority over anything you own. All you have was bought and paid for with the blood of Jesus.

The messages Moses gave to the Israelites did not benefit them. Are we walking as the Israelites? Are we walking in the full power the blood gave to us? When we put anything before God, we are making unto ourselves an idol. In the time of slavery, a slave didn't wear shoes. When Moses removed his shoes, it meant he was relinquishing ownership of all things over to God. He would become a slave unto God. It is time to remove our shoes and take our place, become a vessel unto God. Jesus brought the gospel of God to us in a pure way. He brought to us the message of freedom, deliverance of sin and bondage. No more curse. No more bondage. One night with God can change our life!

New Beginning

I was going through something when I couldn't feel God's *presence*, and after church one Sunday night, I fell on my knees and began to cry out to God. The Holy Spirit quickened me to take communion, and as I opened my Bible and began reading Luke and breaking of the bread, I heard the voice of Jesus speak to me. He said that from the time He was conceived in *Mary's* womb, everything in His earthly journey was put in place for Him, from the pitcher of water for washing the disciple's feet to the donkeys. He said, "Go read it again. For this is the way it is for My children. Everything has been prearranged and put in place. All you have to do is step out in faith and begin *your destiny*."

We live in a freshly body, and as long as we live in these earthly bodies, our mind will be the battlefield for Satan. I want to give you a little insight of who our enemy is. The first thing I want to tell you is, he is real. He is also controlling. He is not omnipresent, but he sends his demon spirits.

In Ephesians 6, it gives us a clear vision of who and what he's about. He is very deceitful. He is called many names and comes in many forms. He is called the destroyer and the father of lies. He is the *accuser* of the brethren, a murderer, and he is spiritual death. He is bitterness and strife, condemnation, and fear. He hates God's people and wants to tear down the kingdom of heaven and wear us down. He works constantly to dethrone God's kingdom; 2 Corinthians 4:4 says he is the god of the evil world.

Satan knows he has no power in our spirit realm, but he tries to make us think he does. When we received Jesus as our Lord and Savior, Jesus stripped him of all power. We are now dead with Christ through the cross, and we are victorious because we are spiritually reborn. We are washed in the blood of the Lamb. This is the Word of God, and the devil cannot change the Word; man can't change the Word. His Word has been established! I like to call it the gateway to freedom.

It is easy to be deceived by the enemy if we let him entertain our thoughts. He knows that if he can get our mind off the cross and the resurrection and on the guilt of our past, he has us in the battle. He has to operate in the natural realm of the soul. He does this through the flesh by way of our mind through deception; this is one of his main tools. He has no new strategies, so he uses the same lies. How many times have you fought the same battle over and over?

Our mind is a memory box where our past lives. It holds the visions of our faults and failures and the images we have created of ourselves. It influences our daily walk by reminding us where we came from, which influences both the consciousness and unconsciousness of man. This is the battlefield of our spiritual warfare, where good and evil wars for the human soul. The flesh desires to turn back to the life you lived before you were saved. I would say it is a lusting spirit for pleasure, control, wickedness, adultery, and manipulation to get the "fine things it desires" no matter who gets hurt or what it has to do to get the power to rule over the natural man's soul.

It is the vision of our past that God no longer sees once the blood has been applied. The devil takes our image of who we were and builds a stronghold in our mind to keep us from becoming all that *God created* us to be. One of his most powerful weapons is anger. Anger causes division in relationships and marriages. It is the opposite of love; it is hate, which causes bitterness. It is all sin, and sin causes spiritual death, *sickness*, and physical death. Gossip is another power tool. Gossip is indulging in idle talk that is rumors about others that causes strife, confusion, and judgment. When we judge someone, it can affect how someone else looks at this person, causing their testimony or ministry not to be received. This will open the door for the enemy to begin judgment upon ourselves.

Judgment takes us out from under grace and places us under the law, where we will only find condemnation, and makes us feel all alone in the battle because our faith has been pushed back. Then depression and oppression take over because we have opened up our mind for the enemy to build a house for the demons to dwell in and the enemy's voice to take over. Then comes in the spirit of unworthiness, and we say over and over, "Lord, I am so unworthy, please forgive me." It is like a worn-out record to God, and all the time, He is saying, "What are you talking about? All I see is My Son's blood."

Before we can pass over to our Jordan, or our Canaan land, we must break these chains of unworthiness. This is a lie from Satan himself. Don't deny the blood! We have yet to pull down our sinful nature or our flesh, the old man, and our old thinking patterns. Pull down all the wrong thoughts from our memory box and demand the demon to leave; shut the door and never open it again. Remove the devil's weapons. Then the Holy Spirit can plunder Satan's house. Remove the thought patterns of what our parents said we were and have a refreshed mind, knowing that we are intelligent women and men of God.

We are adopted into a new life when we're born again, having a new heart, mind, nature, and spirit; all things are made new. We have received the very Spirit of *God* and, through this Spirit, birthed into His heavenly kingdom. We are bone of His bones and flesh of His flesh, joined together through Christ. We have a new Father that will never leave us, never put us down. Begin to see yourself in His image, His likeness, and intelligence. Not only do we have a new life, but we have new hope without limitations on what we can conquer through Christ.

We may get in the season when we can't feel God's presence and think, "Where are you, Lord?" We may feel the old enemy's sword pricking our heart in these seasons and feel like we will begin to bleed and die anytime. You hear the message of deliverance, but we are thinking, "Where is it?" Let me assure you: "For those who are with us are more than those who are with them" (2 Kings 6:16). In this, it is the time to walk by faith and not by sight. It is the time to begin your march in Jesus's name. Speak Jesus's name over the adversary, over your health and *finances.*

"For we wrestle not against flesh and blood but against powers, against the rulers of darkness of the world, against spiritual wickedness in high places." Our battles are with jealousy, bitterness, and unforgiveness. See ourselves not worthy of God's promises (Ephesians 6:12).

The flesh is of the world; it causes discord. It is the foundation of all evil. "But if you have bitter jealousy and selfish ambition in your hearts, do not be arrogant and so to lie against the truth. This wisdom is not that which comes down from above, but earthly, natural, demonic" (James 3:14–15).

"Now the deeds of the flesh are evident which are immorality, idolatry, saucers, strife, jealousy, drunkenness" (Galatians 5:19). Any of these are tools of the enemy. They will destroy and will become infectious if left unattended. Worry is of the flesh, as is feeling unworthy and feeling rejected. I'm not saying we are all sinners; we are not. I'm trying to open your eyes to how the Father sees us through His Son's blood. When we realize Satan has been defeated and put up a No Trespassing sign, only then will we walk in freedom.

Most ladies I have ministered to have been in battles within their minds from past sins. Who is this? It is the accuser of the brother. When we have pure love, it will be easy to forget our past and apply the blood over the faults we see within ourselves and see deliverance. I like to help them by telling them to close their eyes and see a room filled with cabinets and all their past in those cabinets. Walk out the door, shutting it behind you. Look back once, and see the blood over the door. Then turn and walk away, never to be remembered again. Get rid of that fleshly part and walk in the peace of God's love, finding confidence and assurance of His love.

Jealousy causes bitterness; bitterness causes sickness, "which will rot your bones." It will take the *confidence* of who you are in Christ Jesus, causing doubt. Any of these tools will control you, building up strongholds in your mind, letting Satan enter your emotions. God wants us to walk out of the image of condemnation and fear that the devil has created in our mind. We need to be aware of the enemy, resist him, and cast him down. "Resist the devil, and he will flee." Start creating God's image of who His Word tells us we are. We are saved, filled with the Holy Spirit and in the likeness of Christ because He loves us dearly. We are made in His own image. We are of His own creation. This Spirit born within us, the Holy Spirit, helps us grow in the likeness of God and always assures we can receive every promise God has given. We must let God's Word be the ruler of our life, heart, and mind, as Jesus is so also are we in the world.

He who is born of God keeps us and the evil one does not touch us. The place of rest for us is knowing that Jesus paid the price for us to have the right to enter the throne room. Your peace is assured in the love God has for you. You are worthy of His love. It is nothing we've done or can do but what Jesus has already done. Pull down the stronghold of unbelief because Jesus defeated the devil. Believe in the whole salvation plan of the cross and His resurrection and know that the battle has already been won. Don't take on the care of the battle, and the devil will walk away. You are that person being redeemed by the blood of Christ, having victory when Jesus surrendered to the cross.

The way to victory is through God's Word and learning the reason Jesus went to the cross, for our salvation, gives us a newness of life and the gateway to freedom. Through Jesus, we are no longer in bondage to Satan, and every provision for our life is given. His Word is our armor and strength when we are worn and feel defeated. "For I have satiated the weary soul, and I have replenished every sorrowful soul. After this I awake and looked around, and my sleep was sweet to me" (Jeremiah 31:25–26).

Satiated is defined as having satisfied fully or to excess. *Weary* is a term used too often in today's conversation; however, its meaning has not changed! It means to be worn out in strength, energy, or freshness. Jeremiah was being told about the return of Israel as it related to Judah. This was a trying time, and Jeremiah knew it would take a miracle for the return to occur. However, God was imparting the plan to Jeremiah. God not only thought about the provision; He also considered the limitations of the people. He knew Israel was weary, frustrated, and mourning and that a new strength was needed.

God also knows the state of our mind and spirit today. We will have a continuous battle if we keep our mind full of life's daily occurrences, not empty our minds, and renew it with God's Word. We often become short on patience and have signs of exhaustion. This is where the strongholds begin to build in the house of thoughts. What a joy it is for God to satiate your weary soul and replenish your sorrowful soul. Jesus has covered us, so pull down the strongholds, shake it off, and move forward. "For though we walk in the flesh, we do not war according to the flesh. For the weapons of our warfare are not carnal, but mighty in God, for casting down arguments and every high thing that exalts itself against the knowledge of God" (2 Corinthians 10:3–5). Taking our thoughts captive enslaves them to God; but if we don't, then we enslave them to the enemy. That's when he vandalizes your mind. The definition for *captive* is one held in confinement, prison. That is why we should take them captive and let God hold them and replace them with His peace and joy.

We are in constant warfare, and Satan knows our mind is the only ground for our battles. It began in the Garden of Eden when he deceived Eve and she took the first bite of the fruit. Our problem is, we take the thoughts he puts into our mind and let them take root as Eve did; she acted upon the word of her enemy. Anything that edifies our enemy is sin and makes him master of our walk. We have to pull down the strongholds and crucify our fleshly nature, thus removing the tools he uses to do battle.

We have to get in agreement with God's Word and apply it daily to our walk. A vital key is not receiving what Satan says we are but who God says we are. When Satan accuses, do not agree with him but let him know you have been washed in the blood of the Lamb; Jesus is now your master, and you are washed and renewed in body, soul, and spirit.

I am telling you, this works! This is how I came out of my battle of being sexually abused as a child. I thought it was my fault that I was abused and that I had done something to cause it. I thought He would not forgive me because I had been married before and that I was surely headed to hell. I had a very hard time with this until I got into God's Word and fell in love with Him and learned of His grace. I learned of what Jesus's blood did for me and that God is an all-knowing God. Sometimes when we marry out of God's plan for our life; we are "unequally yoked." God knows if that person will receive Jesus as Lord over their life. I'm not telling anyone to get divorced, but

I'm saying if we have had too or have too, we have not committed an unforgivable sin. If I had not divorced, I would not have met my wonderful Christian husband that I now have. I am now covered with his prayers that help me in my walk, and I have learned to trust in God's Word.

Each time Satan looks at us, he is reminded of the battle he lost after the cross and resurrection. He knows the power we walk in even more than we do. He knows if he can keep us from seeing the truth of God's Word that his demons are subject to us in the name of Jesus. "And the seventy returned again with joy saying, "Lord even the demons are subject to us through Your Name" (Luke 10:17).

It is easy to live a sinful life; there are no battles to fight. But when we are wholly committed to God, many are battles until we see ourselves in the likeness of Christ. We have to get hold of this, or the enemy will rob us of our benefits of the cross. He knows that John 14:12 tells us, "Verily, verily, I say unto you, He that believeth on Me, the works that I do shall he do also; and greater works than these shall he do; because I go to the Father." Can you imagine the damage we can do to the evil world? Can't you see why he doesn't want us to win?

Our minds have to be renewed daily by the washing of the water of God's Word standing strong in all He has given us. We have to begin with digesting His Word. When we don't, we get in trouble. A stream of water can't flow if it is damned up. Romans 12:1–2 states, "I beseech you Brother by the mercies of God that you present yourselves as a Living Sacrifice, holy and be not conformed to the world, but be ye transformed by the renewing of your mind that you may prove what is that good and acceptable and perfect will of God."

God wants to birth His spiritual power upon this earth like no man has ever experienced before. He is calling us out. He wants to use us women to do this, knowing that we will birth things into existence. We have been through the labor pains; we've already travailed. We are steadfast, we will pray, and we don't give up.

He reminded me of a little lady in the Bible that kept going before the judge until he told them to give her what she wanted. And there was the lady who gave the two mites; Jesus said she gave all. He knows we will give all we have, and because of this, he will use women in this time and season. It was women who spread the greatest message: "He is risen!" I believe we are in the last stage of the kingdom when Jesus will come. Because of this, we have to make sure our lamps are full and our wicks trimmed and ready to go when He calls.

Back during the war, it was the women who prayed. I can still hear their voices as they cried out to the Father for our men in America. We have to cry out for America today before we have a spiritual downfall. When we remove God from our nation, we are in trouble.

God is calling us into a new beginning. We have to walk out of the principalities of the darkness of our mind, pull down the strongholds, and say no to the devil. Kick him out and walk in the light of Christ! We are weak within ourselves, but we are made strong through Christ Jesus. We are more than conquerors through Christ Jesus. We are the head and not the tail, above and not beneath.

God's Word is the direction for our journey. It is the pathway to freedom. Living without His Word is like traveling on a journey without a map. We are lost! God's Word sets a standard against our enemy. Isaiah 59:19 states, "So shall they revere the name of the Lord from the West and His glory from the rising of the sun. For the oppressor shall come like a flood, and the Spirit of the Lord shall humble him." This scripture tells us that the victory over our battles is already won. No matter what it looks like, look to the east, toward the rising of the Son (Messiah); our journey is almost over. God wants to get His bride ready for the homecoming, the wedding feast.

Ask God to give you wisdom for decisions and comfort in your distresses and help you cling to the purpose of Jesus's blood that was shed on the cross. Look to Jesus, the Author and Finisher of our faith. I believe He is asking us in this scripture, "What do you have the faith for Me to do in your life?"

As Cain killed Abel and his blood cried out from the ground, Jesus's blood cries out to the Father for us today. His blood declares victory over Satan, over our battles. The more we see ourselves sprinkled with His blood, the more we will see ourselves free. The more we see ourselves dead in Christ because of the cross, the more likely that the door to a victorious life will be ours. I'm telling you, the devil will run when he sees us coming!

The spirits we fight does not have a body to walk in full power. If we do not see ourselves covered by the blood and worthy of it, they can attach themselves. I want to ask you something. How do your battles begin? They begin by one thought the devil plants in our mind and entertaining that thought.

The Father gave His Son as the sacrifice, and His blood atoned for us. I believe it saddens His heart when we don't see ourselves worthy to receive the gifts He gives. We are all His children, He loves us, and we belong to Him. We are called to God's kingdom. Who dares to enter the King's court and take anything that belongs to the King of kings? We abide under the shadow of the Almighty God. There is a place in God in the spiritual realm where our spirits are fully saturated with the living presence of the glory of the Lord Jesus. We can go into his presence, and the enemy can't even smell us. We have a fortress that keeps us from any arrow the enemy may shoot; we are hidden from all evil. Remember Psalm 91: "He who dwells in the secret place of the Most High shall abide under the shadow of the Almighty! I will say of the Lord, He is my rock, my refuge, my fortress."

He awoke me one morning, reminding me of Job, "Think about Job when Satan came before Me. I asked him where he had been. Satan answered, 'From going to and fro in the Earth, and from walking up and down in it.' God asked, 'Have you considered my servant Job, that there is none like him on earth, a perfect and upright man?' Satan answered, 'You have a hedge about him.'" God said, "This same hedge is about you. Nothing can harm you, and nothing can come near you that I don't allow. If I allow it, you will be victorious." Every need we have has been provided for us on the cross.

I believe He asked this: "Will you walk in My freedom? Will you lie all down and receive My sacrifice?" It is only through faith that we can do what He asks. Faith comes by hearing, hearing by the Word of God. Faith is the substance of things hoped for, the evidence of things not seen. Faith believes I have the promises of God now and that I am victorious in my battles and my sins are buried with Jesus in the tomb. The same Spirit that raised Jesus from the dead lives in me. I must not walk by the way I feel but by faith and not by sight. I call those things be not though they were. I'm telling you, your faith will never rise higher than your confession. Let us walk anew, putting Jesus first in our life.

Paul fought many battles. He was beaten, put in prison, and took thirty-nine stripes five times. But he never wavered or fainted; he walked each step by faith. He refused to look back from where he came, only looking ahead, where Jesus was taking him. He never complained about the beatings or imprisonment. He knew that Jesus had already walked the journey and cleared the way. He had only to endure the pain; so don't waver or faint during your preparation for the new beginning God is taking you to. We have only to rise up in faith and step out. A seeking heart will always find the Lord, and salvation will come.

David told Solomon in 1 Chronicles 28:9, "And you Solomon my son know thou the God of your father, and serve Him with a perfect heart and with a willing mind: for the Lord searches all hearts, and understands all the imaginations of the thoughts: if you seek Him, He will be found of you; but if you forsake Him, He will cast you off for ever."

Before the children of Egypt could go through the Red Sea, they had to step out and move up to where God was calling them. If they had not taken this first step, they would not have walked out of Egypt. No devil or person can separate us from God. Our past can't and will not. Don't let the devil entertain your thoughts, making you believe you are anything less than God's Word says you are. He has made a way out of our shortcomings as long as we repent from our sins and turn away.

Jesus asked His disciples, "'Whom do man say that I, the Son, of man am?' And they said, 'some say John the Baptist: Some Elijah, and others Jeremiah, or one of the prophets.' He said unto them 'Whom do you say that I am?' and Peter answered and said unto Him, 'You are the Christ, the Son of the Living God.' And Jesus answered and said unto him, 'Blessed are thou, Simon Bar-jona: for flesh and blood have not revealed it to thee, by My, Father which are in Heaven and I say unto thee. That thou art Peter, and upon this rock I will build My Church; and the gates of hell shall not prevail, against it. And I will give unto thee the keys of the Kingdom of Heaven'" (Matthew 16:13–19).

Even though Jesus knew that later He would have to rebuke Peter and call him Satan and that Peter would deny Him not once but three times, He did not hold out His hand and say, "Give Me the keys back, boy. You messed up." This is the same God we serve today, and when we mess up, He'll not hold out His hand and say, "Give Me My Son's blood back, you messed up." He will pick us up after repentance and wash us off and putting us back on the path of righteousness. This is the Father's word for us.

I ask you, "Should we be the ones to cower down and be oppressed, walking in condemnation with our heads bowed down?" The Holy Spirit speaks to us deep in our heart and tells us that we really are God's children and we share in His treasures and all God gives to His Son is now ours. This scripture you will find in Romans.

I want to show you something: take something black and look at it. This is our life in sin. Now take a book as though it was a book of records and every sin you have committed is written in that book. Now picture Jesus taking a towel and dipping it into His blood, wiping each page clean. Now take something white and look at it. Where are your sins? They have been removed, thrown into the sea of forgetfulness, never to wash upon memory's shore. "I, even I, am He who blots out your transgressions for My Own sake, and will not remember your sin" (Isaiah 43:25).

Let us arise and shine, for this is our season for new beginnings. This is our time and season for birth. He is waiting for us to make the first step to "commitment." Then only will He take us through the Red Sea.

God is always attentive to your needs. He will never fail us. His eyes are always upon us, seeking ways to please us. He loves to find ways to bless us. We are the ones who open the door through sin for the enemy to keep us from walking in the gifts the Father has given to each of us. Where there is sin, there is darkness, and darkness is where Satan has a legal right to tread those areas, given to him by God. We must stay out of the dark places and walk in the light of Jesus.

When we become satisfied with our spiritual walk and sit down, never opening our Bibles, not attending church, we let the enemy bind our march and invade our relationship with God. We can't stand still! We have to get up and take control of our place in God. If we have ever known God, it is the time to hold to His promises and not look back from where we come.

Take a look at all the things that are taking place in the world: fires, mud slides… And don't forget 9/11. We must return to our first love, never removing our eyes from the cross and resurrection. I believe we have walked ahead of God. We have gotten so busy we forget to take time for God. Let us run our race of life with our eyes firmly fixed upon Jesus.

God wants to heal our heart. We have to expose the scars that we can't let heal because of something from the past that we think we've hidden from God. When we expose our darkest secrets and bring them into the light, the condemnation, fear, and unworthiness the devil has created will be healed. We have been born with Christ through the Spirit of God. Now that we know His nature and begin to walk in His image and likeness, we can grow in God, always assured we can receive the blessings and promises. We must let God's Word be the ruler of our flesh, heart, and mind. As He is also are we in the world, and he who was born of God keep us and the evil one does not touch us.

We have to fill our atmosphere with good thoughts about ourselves. God doesn't want us to be afraid to bring our sins to Him. He already knows anyhow. He wants us to expose the things the devil keeps picking us with. He is a God of peace. When we expose the devil by bringing our secrets in the light, the devil will walk away and God can heal us. The devil cannot use anything that is uncovered and brought into the light.

We have to make God's Word the final authority over all conditions and circumstances that are contrary to His Word. Let's put His Word in front of our walk. We are destined and appointed by

God to become progressive in knowing His will for our life, which is His Word. I have heard so many people say I don't know what God's will is for my life. His will for us is anything Jesus went to the cross for, anything His Word tells us we have. We have to let His Word be active in us through the Holy Spirit. When He died for us, it assured us that we have what He says we have, whatever we have the faith to receive. The more we speak His Word, the stronger our faith becomes. We have to know the truth of His Word and become rooted in His truths. His truth is our hope. We have the hope that His truth within us will make us free.

Faith will bring the things He says we have into existence in our life now. Faith and hope go hand in hand; if you have faith, you can move God. Faith is taking God's Word and applying it to every circumstance and seeing the end result—not the present lack, sickness, or bondage and putting up with it.

I have heard people say, "Lord, if it be, thy will heal me." His will is for us to be healed. Why the stripes on Jesus's back? Did He go to the whipping post for nothing? Didn't He die so that we would have these things after death? His Word tells us that after our death, we will walk on streets of purest gold, no more sickness, no more tears—a new body!

We have been taught that we are unworthy and couldn't become righteous enough for us to walk with God in the place He desires to move us into. I can't tell you how many times I prayed over and over for God to forgive me of the same sin until I received the revelation of His Word. When we receive Jesus as our Lord and Savior, He birthed His righteousness in us. His Word tells us to walk in a God kind of love, to endure long and patiently and to be kind. We are to never be envious and never boil over with jealousy. We are not to display ourselves haughtily, not to be boastful, rude, or vain. We are not to insist in our own ways, living the way we choose.

Jerusalem became a prostitute to other countries around her. She sold herself to other gods. When we flirt with the devil and his demons, we get into trouble. Satan will raise his ugly head and consume you. Look at Saul and the tormenting spirits he dealt with because of his flesh. When we die to self, there *is no* legal right for the attacks. We have to keep our life lined up with the Word of God and His commandments in order to live a victorious life.

Our path of life is only a decision we have to make to usher us into the life God has chosen for us. The trials and temptations we have endured, Jesus already walked through these before us as He did Paul. We are to rejoice when righteousness and truth prevail. We are to be peacemakers. We are to turn from idle words and foolish things that are contrary to our true desires toward others. His Word is spirit and life. God's ability is released in us through the Word of God. We must give ear to His Word and not let them depart from our sight but keep them in the midst of our heart, for they are healing to our bones. We must believe He lives at the Father's right hand, making intercessions for us; we are covered. For those who don't believe the full scriptures of Mark 16:16, "they are condemned."

God told Noah, "The end of the flesh has come." He told Noah to build an ark. For 125 years, Noah preached the same message: "It is going to rain." Because they had never seen rain, they had a hard time believing this message, but the floods came. No one but Noah and his family was saved. The people in that time laughed at Noah. Do you laugh at the one that tells you today that Jesus is coming?

Are you going to be left behind when this great event takes place? "And behold, Jesus is coming quickly. Blessed is he who heeds the words of the prophecy of this book" (Revelation 22:7). We have to stay close to God by staying in His Word and do what it tells us to do. I believe the closer it gets to His coming, the easier it will be to be deceived. Not one of the disciples knew that Judas would betray Jesus; they walked with him every day. The Word tells us that Satan himself is transformed into an angel of light. Don't let the enemy deceive you in this time and season. Jesus is coming! Receive the salvation plan that Jesus paid the price for us to have, cast out the enemy, rise up in victory of who you are because of the blood that was shed at Calvary, and receive your new beginning.

About the Author

 Betsy has been married for twenty years and has one child of her own and two stepchildren, who are all grown. She has lived in Alabama all her life, where she has ministered to women at her church, conducted home Bible studies, mentored, participated in the Christian Women's Job Corps, and gone wherever He has placed her through the years. Her prayer has always been to minister to hurting women and to help them know God.